STROKE AND
HEART DISEASE

GENERAL EDITORS

Dale C. Garell, M.D.

Medical Director, California Children Services, Department of Health
    Services, County of Los Angeles
Associate Dean for Curriculum
Clinical Professor, Department of Pediatrics & Family Medicine,
    University of Southern California School of Medicine
Former President, Society for Adolescent Medicine

Solomon H. Snyder, M.D.

Distinguished Service Professor of Neuroscience, Pharmacology, and
    Psychiatry, Johns Hopkins University School of Medicine
Former president, Society of Neuroscience
Albert Lasker Award in Medical Research, 1978

CONSULTING EDITORS

Robert W. Blum, M.D., Ph.D.

Associate Professor, School of Public Health and Department of
    Pediatrics
Director, Adolescent Health Program, University of Minnesota
    Consultant, World Health Organization

Charles E. Irwin, Jr., M.D.

Associate Professor of Pediatrics; Director, Division of Adolescent
    Medicine, University of California, San Francisco

Lloyd J. Kolbe, Ph.D.

Chief, Office of School Health & Special Projects, Center for Health
    Promotion & Education, Centers for Disease Control
President, American School Health Association

Jordan J. Popkin

Director, Division of Federal Employee Occupational Health, U.S. Public
    Health Service Region I

Joseph L. Rauh, M.D.

Professor of Pediatrics and Medicine, Adolescent Medicine, Children's
    Hospital Medical Center, Cincinnati
Former president, Society for Adolescent Medicine

THE ENCYCLOPEDIA OF
H E A L T H

MEDICAL DISORDERS
AND THEIR TREATMENT

Dale C. Garell, M.D. · General Editor

STROKE AND HEART DISEASE

Anne Galperin

Introduction by C. Everett Koop, M.D., Sc.D.
former Surgeon General, U.S. Public Health Service

CHELSEA HOUSE PUBLISHERS
New York · Philadelphia

ON THE COVER An illustration of the human heart by Eileen McKeating. Derived from "Das Herz des Menschen" in *Traité complet de l'anatomie de l'homme* by Nach Bourgery.

Chelsea House Publishers
EDITOR-IN-CHIEF Remmel Nunn
MANAGING EDITOR Karyn Gullen Browne
COPY CHIEF Juliann Barbato
PICTURE EDITOR Adrian G. Allen
ART DIRECTOR Maria Epes
DEPUTY COPY CHIEF Mark Rifkin
ASSISTANT ART DIRECTOR Loraine Machlin
MANUFACTURING MANAGER Gerald Levine
SYSTEMS MANAGER Rachel Vigier
PRODUCTION MANAGER Joseph Romano
PRODUCTION COORDINATOR Marie Claire Cebrián

The Encyclopedia of Health
SENIOR EDITOR Paula Edelson

Staff for STROKE AND HEART DISEASE
ASSOCIATE EDITOR Will Broaddus
COPY EDITOR Karen Hammonds
EDITORIAL ASSISTANT Leigh Hope Wood
PICTURE RESEARCHER Diana Gongora
SENIOR DESIGNER Marjorie Zaum
DESIGN ASSISTANT Debora Smith

3 5 7 9 8 6 4

Library of Congress Cataloging-in-Publication Data

Galperin, Anne.
  Stroke and heart disease / Anne Galperin.
    p. cm.—(The Encyclopedia of health)
  Includes bibliographical references.
  Summary: Describes the basic features of the heart and cardiovascular system, the diseases that may affect them, and the science that has evolved to treat heart diseases.
  ISBN 0-7910-0077-X
      0-7910-0505-4 (pbk.)
  1. Cardiovascular system—Diseases—Juvenile literature. 2. Cerebrovascular disease—Juvenile literature. [1. Heart. 2. Heart—Diseases. 3. Circulatory system. 4. Circulatory system—Diseases.] I. Title. II. Series.   89-13922
RC667.G35 1990   CIP
616.1—dc20   AC

CONTENTS

The goal of the ENCYCLOPEDIA OF HEALTH *is to provide general information in the ever-changing areas of physiology, psychology, and related medical issues. The titles in this series are not intended to take the place of the professional advice of a physician or other health care professional.*

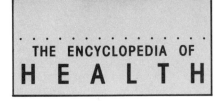

THE ENCYCLOPEDIA OF

H E A L T H

PREVENTION AND EDUCATION: THE KEYS TO GOOD HEALTH

C. Everett Koop, M.D., Sc.D.
former Surgeon General,
U.S. Public Health Service

The issue of health education has received particular attention in recent years because of the presence of AIDS in the news. But our response to this particular tragedy points up a number of broader issues that doctors, public health officials, educators, and the public face. In particular, it points up the necessity for sound health education for citizens of all ages.

Over the past 25 years this country has been able to bring about dramatic declines in the death rates for heart disease, stroke, accidents, and, for people under the age of 45, cancer. Today, Americans generally eat better and take better care of themselves than ever before. Thus, with the help of modern science and technology, they have a better chance of surviving serious—even catastrophic—illnesses. That's the good news.

But, like every phonograph record, there's a flip side, and one with special significance for young adults. According to a report issued in 1979 by Dr. Julius Richmond, my predecessor as Surgeon General, Americans aged 15 to 24 had a higher death rate in 1979 than they did 20 years earlier. The causes: violent death and injury, alcohol and drug abuse, unwanted pregnancies, and sexually transmitted diseases. Adolescents are particularly vulnerable because they are beginning to explore their own sexuality and perhaps to experiment with drugs. The need for educating young people is critical, and the price of neglect is high.

Yet even for the population as a whole, our health is still far from what it could be. Why? A 1974 Canadian government report attributed all death and disease to four broad elements: inadequacies in the health care system, behavioral factors or unhealthy life-styles, environmental hazards, and human biological factors.

To be sure, there are diseases that are still beyond the control of even our advanced medical knowledge and techniques. And despite yearnings that are as old as the human race itself, there is no "fountain of youth" to ward off aging and death. Still, there is a solution to many of the problems that undermine sound health. In a word, that solution is prevention. Prevention, which includes health promotion and education, saves lives, improves the quality of life, and, in the long run, saves money.

In the United States, organized public health activities and preventive medicine have a long history. Important milestones include the improvement of sanitary procedures and the development of pasteurized milk in the late 19th century, and the introduction in the mid-20th century of effective vaccines against polio, measles, German measles, mumps, and other once-rampant diseases. Internationally, organized public health efforts began on a wide-scale basis with the International Sanitary Conference of 1851, to which 12 nations sent representatives. The World Health Organization, founded in 1948, continues these efforts under the aegis of the United Nations, with particular emphasis on combatting communicable diseases and the training of health care workers.

Despite these accomplishments, much remains to be done in the field of prevention. For too long, we have had a medical care system that is science- and technology-based, focused, essentially, on illness and mortality. It is now patently obvious that both the social and the economic costs of such a system are becoming insupportable.

Implementing prevention—and its corollaries, health education and promotion—is the job of several groups of people.

First, the medical and scientific professions need to continue basic scientific research, and here we are making considerable progress. But increased concern with prevention will also have a decided impact on how primary care doctors practice medicine. With a shift to health-based rather than morbidity-based medicine, the role of the "new physician" will include a healthy dose of patient education.

Second, practitioners of the social and behavioral sciences—psychologists, economists, city planners—along with lawyers, business leaders, and government officials—must solve the practical and ethical dilemmas confronting us: poverty, crime, civil rights, literacy, education, employment, housing, sanitation, environmental protection, health care delivery systems, and so forth. All of these issues affect public health.

Third is the public at large. We'll consider that very important group in a moment.

Fourth, and the linchpin in this effort, is the public health profession—doctors, epidemiologists, teachers—who must harness the professional expertise of the first two groups and the common sense and cooperation of the third, the public. They must define the problems statistically and qualitatively and then help us set priorities for finding the solutions.

To a very large extent, improving those statistics is the responsibility of every individual. So let's consider more specifically what the role of the individual should be and why health education is so important to that role. First, and most obviously, individuals can protect themselves from illness and injury and thus minimize their need for professional medical care. They can eat nutritious food, get adequate exercise, avoid tobacco, alcohol, and drugs, and take prudent steps to avoid accidents. The proverbial "apple a day keeps the doctor away" is not so far from the truth, after all.

Second, individuals should actively participate in their own medical care. They should schedule regular medical and dental checkups. Should they develop an illness or injury, they should know when to treat themselves and when to seek professional help. To gain the maximum benefit from any medical treatment that they do require, individuals must become partners in that treatment. For instance, they should understand the effects and side effects of medications. I counsel young physicians that there is no such thing as too much information when talking with patients. But the corollary is the patient must know enough about the nuts and bolts of the healing process to understand what the doctor is telling him. That is at least partially the patient's responsibility.

Education is equally necessary for us to understand the ethical and public policy issues in health care today. Sometimes individuals will encounter these issues in making decisions about their own treatment or that of family members. Other citizens may encounter them as jurors in medical malpractice cases. But we all become involved, indirectly, when we elect our public officials, from school board members to the president. Should surrogate parenting be legal? To what extent is drug testing desirable, legal, or necessary? Should there be public funding for family planning, hospitals, various types of medical research, and medical care for the indigent? How should we allocate scant technological resources, such as kidney dialysis and organ transplants? What is the proper role of government in protecting the rights of patients?

What are the broad goals of public health in the United States today? In 1980, the Public Health Service issued a report aptly entitled *Promoting Health—Preventing Disease: Objectives for the Nation.* This report expressed its goals in terms of mortality and in terms of intermediate goals in education and health improvement. It identified 15 major concerns: controlling high blood pressure; improving family planning; improving pregnancy care and infant health; increasing the rate of immunization; controlling sexually transmitted diseases; controlling the presence of toxic agents and radiation in the environment; improving occupational safety and health; preventing accidents; promoting water fluoridation and dental health; controlling infectious diseases; decreasing smoking; decreasing alcohol and drug abuse; improving nutrition; promoting physical fitness and exercise; and controlling stress and violent behavior.

For healthy adolescents and young adults (ages 15 to 24), the specific goal was a 20% reduction in deaths, with a special focus on motor vehicle injuries and alcohol and drug abuse. For adults (ages 25 to 64), the aim was 25% fewer deaths, with a concentration on heart attacks, strokes, and cancers.

Smoking is perhaps the best example of how individual behavior can have a direct impact on health. Today cigarette smoking is recognized as the most important single preventable cause of death in our society. It is responsible for more cancers and more cancer deaths than any other known agent; is a prime risk factor for heart and blood vessel disease, chronic bronchitis, and emphysema; and is a frequent cause of complications in pregnancies and of babies born prematurely, underweight, or with potentially fatal respiratory and cardiovascular problems.

Since the release of the Surgeon General's first report on smoking in 1964, the proportion of adult smokers has declined substantially, from 43% in 1965 to 30.5% in 1985. Since 1965, 37 million people have quit smoking. Although there is still much work to be done if we are to become a "smoke-free society," it is heartening to note that public health and public education efforts—such as warnings on cigarette packages and bans on broadcast advertising—have already had significant effects.

In 1835, Alexis de Tocqueville, a French visitor to America, wrote, "In America the passion for physical well-being is general." Today, as then, health and fitness are front-page items. But with the greater scientific and technological resources now available to us, we are in a far stronger position to make good health care available to everyone. And with the greater technological threats to us as we approach the 21st century, the need to do so is more urgent than ever before. Comprehensive information about basic biology, preventive medicine, medical and surgical treatments, and related ethical and public policy issues can help you arm yourself with the knowledge you need to be healthy throughout your life.

FOREWORD

Dale C. Garell, M.D.

Advances in our understanding of health and disease during the 20th century have been truly remarkable. Indeed, it could be argued that modern health care is one of the greatest accomplishments in all of human history. In the early 1900s, improvements in sanitation, water treatment, and sewage disposal reduced death rates and increased longevity. Previously untreatable illnesses can now be managed with antibiotics, immunizations, and modern surgical techniques. Discoveries in the fields of immunology, genetic diagnosis, and organ transplantation are revolutionizing the prevention and treatment of disease. Modern medicine is even making inroads against cancer and heart disease, two of the leading causes of death in the United States.

Although there is much to be proud of, medicine continues to face enormous challenges. Science has vanquished diseases such as smallpox and polio, but new killers, most notably AIDS, confront us. Moreover, we now victimize ourselves with what some have called "diseases of choice," or those brought on by drug and alcohol abuse, bad eating habits, and mismanagement of the stresses and strains of contemporary life. The very technology that is doing so much to prolong life has brought with it previously unimaginable ethical dilemmas related to issues of death and dying. The rising cost of health care is a matter of central concern to us all. And violence in the form of automobile accidents, homicide, and suicide remains the major killer of young adults.

In the past, most people were content to leave health care and medical treatment in the hands of professionals. But since the 1960s, the consumer of medical care—that is, the patient—has assumed an increasingly central role in the management of his or her own health. There has also been a new emphasis placed on prevention: People are recognizing that their own actions can help prevent many of the conditions that have caused death and disease in the past. This accounts for the growing commitment to good nutrition and regular exercise, for the fact that more and more people are choosing not to smoke, and for a new moderation in people's drinking habits.

People want to know more about themselves and their own health. They are curious about their body: its anatomy, physiology, and biochemistry. They want to keep up with rapidly evolving medical technologies and procedures. They are willing to educate themselves about common disorders and diseases so that they can be full partners in their own health care.

The ENCYCLOPEDIA OF HEALTH is designed to provide the basic knowledge that readers will need if they are to take significant responsibility for their own health. It is also meant to serve as a frame of reference for further study and exploration. The ENCYCLOPEDIA is divided into five subsections: The Healthy Body; the Life Cycle; Medical Disorders & Their Treatment; Psychological Disorders & Their Treatment; and Medical Issues. For each topic covered by the ENCYCLOPEDIA, we present the essential facts about the relevant biology; the symptoms, diagnosis, and treatment of common diseases and disorders; and ways in which you can prevent or reduce the severity of health problems when that is possible. The ENCYCLOPEDIA also projects what may lie ahead in the way of future treatment or prevention strategies.

The broad range of topics and issues covered in the ENCYCLOPEDIA reflects the fact that human health encompasses physical, psychological, social, environmental, and spiritual well-being. Just as the mind and the body are inextricably linked, so, too, is the individual an integral part of the wider world that comprises his or her family, society, and environment. To discuss health in its broadest aspect it is necessary to explore the many ways in which it is connected to such fields as law, social science, public policy, economics, and even religion. And so, the ENCYCLOPEDIA is meant to be a bridge between science, medical technology, the world at large, and you. I hope that it will inspire you to pursue in greater depth particular areas of interest and that you will take advantage of the suggestions for further reading and the lists of resources and organizations that can provide additional information.

CHAPTER 1

· · · · · · · · · · · · · ·

THE CIRCULATORY SYSTEM

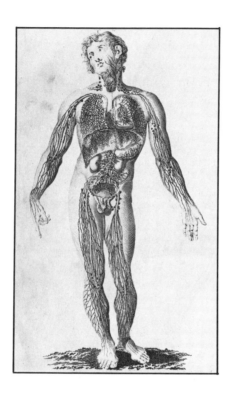

On average, the human heart weighs less than a pound and is rarely much larger than a fist, hardly the size one might expect for an organ that pumps 2,000 gallons of blood through the body each day, never stopping during work, sleep, or exercise. This tireless beating is no protection, however, against cardio-vascular disease—illness of the heart and blood vessels—which kills 1 American every 32 seconds, making it the leading cause of death in the United States. To some extent this high rate of fatality is a natural consequence of the aging process, and with the increased life expectancy imparted by modern medicine, there are now many more potential victims of heart disease. Still, more than 45% of all heart attacks occur in people less than 65 years old, which only adds to the puzzle of why one-quarter of all Americans suffer from cardiovascular disease at some point in their life, whether it be high blood pressure, heart disease, heart attack, or stroke.

Scientists have been able to identify the causes and conditions of almost all of the many types of heart disease, and most explanations for the high incidence of heart disease in America emphasize the many stresses imposed by modern life, from the pressures of the workplace to the emotional worries imposed by poverty to such obvious hazards as poor nutrition and the consumption of alcohol and tobacco. Perhaps the most important fact scientists have discovered about cardiovascular diseases is that they are not necessarily fatal; advances in medical treatment, if accompanied by careful health habits, have been proven to go a long way toward controlling, curing, and preventing cardiovascular illness.

THE HEART

Contrary to popular belief, the heart is not really on the left side of the body but actually lies near the center of the chest, where it is attached to the breastbone by ligaments; it is only the pulsing bottom tip, the apex of the heart, which tilts toward the left, that beats beneath the left breast.

The heart's walls are composed of three layers, each with a distinct character, texture, and function. *Myocardium*, the middle and thickest layer, is a unique muscle tissue in that it looks like the striated, or striped, tissue found in voluntary muscles—muscles that respond to conscious commands, such as to move an arm or a leg. However, its fibers are far more tightly interwoven than those in voluntary muscles, a feature that ensures that the entire organ will receive electrical signals that reach one part of the heart; this helps coordinate the different functions of a heartbeat.

Surrounding the heart and containing the initial sections of its branching large vessels is a double-layered sac of thick connective tissue called the *pericardium*, a Latin word meaning "around the heart." The inner layer fits snugly around the heart, then at its bottom tip doubles back over itself to form the loose outer sac. The space between these two layers—the pericardial cavity—is filled with a serous, or watery, fluid that permits the pericardium's two layers to slide over each other as the heart contracts, at the same time protecting it from the friction this creates.

The heart is divided into four main chambers, the right and left atria at the top, the right and left ventricles at the bottom. Each chamber is lined with a smooth tissue called endocardium, which eases the flow of blood and minimizes friction. The Latin names—*atrium* means "entrance hall" and *ventriculus* means "little belly"—graphically characterize the function of each chamber: the atria receive blood and direct it into the ventricles, where it is pumped out of the heart.

Valves direct the flow of blood between the chambers and prevent it from flowing backward. The *tricuspid valve*, located between the right atrium and right ventricle, is so named because of its three flaps, or *cusps*. The *mitral valve*, positioned between the left atrium and ventricle, has two flaps that resemble a bishop's pointed hat, or miter. Two other valves regulate blood flow out of the heart: The *aortic valve* connects the left ventricle to a large artery called the *aorta* and the *pulmonary valve* joins the right ventricle with the *pulmonary artery*.

The right and left sides of the heart, separated by a muscular wall called the *septum*, each serve a different function. The left heart is responsible for *systemic circulation*—pumping blood for the entire body—so it is the larger and more muscular side. *Pulmonary circulation*, the cycling of blood back and forth between the heart and lungs, is performed by the right heart.

The one-inch-wide aorta—the artery that carries blood to the body—arches forward from the left ventricle and descends through the chest to the abdomen. Five arteries branch from its peak: two coronary arteries, which supply the heart with oxygenated blood; an innominate artery, which supplies the right side of the head and brain, as well as the right arm; and the *left carotid artery* and *left subclavian artery*, both of which supply blood to the head, neck, and left arm.

THE HEARTBEAT AND
THE CARDIAC CYCLE

Everyone is familiar with the "lub-dub, lub-dub" sound of a heartbeat. The heart beats 100,000 times *each day*, in response to electrical impulses that, 60 to 80 times a minute, are discharged from a small bundle of muscle cells in the wall of the right atrium. This bundle of cells—the heart's natural "pacemaker"—is called the *sinoatrial*, or SA, node, a C-shaped area 10 to 15 millimeters long.

Sympathetic nerves branching from the spinal cord can further stimulate the heart to produce a faster and stronger beat when it is needed, for example during a strenuous run. And the *vagus nerve*, which emerges from the lower part of the brain, can signal the heart to produce slower, less powerful beats when appropriate. But the SA node is the source of the normal heartbeat.

Many events take place during the eight-tenths of a second it takes to complete one cardiac cycle, or heartbeat. During the first half of the cardiac cycle, an electrical impulse from the SA node spreads through the atrial walls to another node, the *atrioventricular*, or AV, node, located close to the septum in the lower left portion of the right atrium. The impulse then travels to the bundle of His and the Purkinje fibers, both clusters of highly conductive nerve fibers that extend through the ventricular walls.

The electrical current branches out and spreads through the inside and outside walls of both ventricles. The heart muscles contract as the impulse spreads from the top to the bottom of the heart: first in the atrial contraction, during which blood is pumped from the atria to the ventricles; then, fractions of a second later, in the ventricular contraction, which pumps blood out of the heart. During the second half of the cardiac cycle, the heart's chambers rest for about four-tenths of a second while the atria refill with more blood for the next contraction.

Though all four of the heart's chambers work hard, the amount of pressure exerted differs with their individual functions and also varies depending on the stage of the cardiac cycle. The range of blood pressures a given heart chamber is subject to throughout the cardiac cycle is called a pressure gradient.

CIRCULATION

When bright red oxygen-rich blood is pumped from the left ventricle to the aorta, then courses through the arteries to all parts of the body, it delivers oxygen and nutrients to the tissues. In return, the tissues discharge carbon dioxide, water, and waste. The veins then carry the blood back to the heart, where the cycle begins again. This depleted blood is visible in the veins underlying the skin of the inner wrist, where its blue color betrays its lack of oxygen.

Veins carrying blood from the top of the body feed into the superior vena cava, and veins from the body's lower half are served by the inferior vena cava. Both funnel blood into the heart through the right atrium, where it passes through the tricuspid valve into the right ventricle. From there it is pumped through the pulmonary valve into the pulmonary artery that leads to the lungs, where carbon dioxide is exchanged for oxygen. And then the cycle—from the left side of the heart out to the body through the arteries, through the veins back to the right heart and lungs, from the lungs back to the heart—begins anew.

Components of the Circulatory System

The network of arteries, veins, and capillaries by which the circulatory system ferries nutrients, oxygen, wastes, salts, hormones, and other substances through the body is more than 60,000 miles in length. Each arterial wall is composed of three layers: the *outer adventitia*, a loose layer of connective tissue; the *media*, or second layer, which is composed of elastic tissue and muscle; and the *intima*, a thin, smooth inner lining. *Arterioles* are small branches of the arteries that extend in a fine network to the surrounding tissue.

Veins, which carry blood back to the heart, branch out into smaller extensions called *venules*. The layers composing each vein correspond roughly in size and function to those found in arteries, except that they are somewhat less durable. Arteries need to be much sturdier than veins because blood leaves the heart having much more force than on its return trip. There is so little pressure in the veins that smaller ones actually have valves to keep blood flowing toward the heart. Capillaries are microscopic

THE CIRCULATORY SYSTEM

1. right atrium
2. left atrium
3. right ventricle
4. left ventricle
5. vena cava superior
6. vena cava inferior
7. pulmonary arteries
8. lungs
9. pulmonary veins
10. aorta
11. alimentary canal
12. liver
13. hepatic artery
14. portal vein
15. hepatic vein

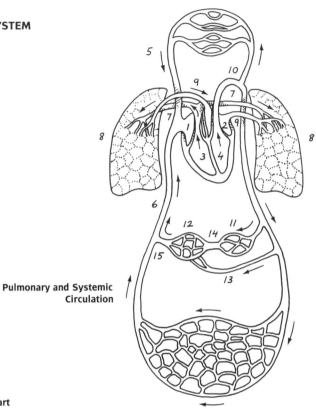

Pulmonary and Systemic Circulation

Circulation Through the Heart

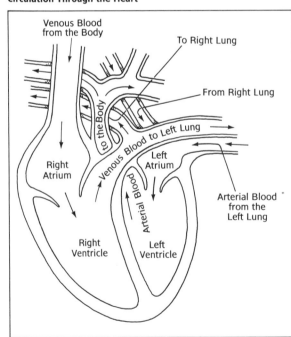

Venous Blood from the Body

To Right Lung

From Right Lung

to the Body

Venous Blood to Left Lung

Arterial Blood

Right Atrium

Left Atrium

Arterial Blood from the Left Lung

Right Ventricle

Left Ventricle

vessels that link arterioles and venules; they are the part of the circulatory system by which oxygen and nutrients, which are carried in the blood, are fed into the body's tissues and by which waste by-products are in turn carried back out of the body.

Cardiac Circulation

The heart receives its own supply of oxygenated blood from the right and left coronary arteries, which branch from the peak of the aorta. A full 10% of the blood the heart pumps makes its way back to the heart muscle by this means. The left coronary arteries split into two branches: The anterior descending branch runs along the front of the heart; and the circumflex branch lies in a groove between the left atrium and ventricle. The right coronary artery fits into the groove between the right atrium and ventricle. It and the circumflex branch form a crown—"crown" is the literal translation of the Latin word *corona*, from which "coronary" is derived—of blood vessels around the heart.

Arterioles branch out from the main arteries and dip into the heart to maintain its blood supply. The right coronary artery feeds both the SA and AV nodes, the right ventricle, and the back of the septum. The front surface and tip of the heart, plus the front of the septum, receive their blood from the anterior descending branch of the left coronary artery. The portion of the left ventricle wall farthest away from the septum receives blood from the circumflex branch of the left coronary artery. Coronary veins drain into a large channel called the coronary sinus, which then empties into the right atrium.

DIAGNOSTIC TESTS
AND HEART FUNCTION

Doctors use many different diagnostic and monitoring techniques to gather information about heart performance. Some, such as measuring blood pressure, listening to the heart with a stethoscope, and performing electrocardiography, are done from outside the body. Invasive methods are those that involve direct access to the heart and blood vessels themselves; among these techniques are cardiac catheterization and angiography. Gathering basic information about heart function by checking blood pressure, listening to the heart, and taking a chest X ray is a standard part of regular checkups. Other techniques are usually performed by or at the request of cardiologists (heart specialists) if heart disorders are suspected.

Noninvasive Techniques

Blood pressure is the force with which the heart and arteries push blood through the body. Blood pressure measurement is one of the quickest, most painless, and most vital medical tests that can be performed. A tool invented in the late 1800s, called a sphygmomanometer—sphygmo, for short—is used to measure blood pressure. The sphygmo consists of a gauge, a cuff, and a pump.

The doctor wraps the cuff around the patient's right arm, places a stethoscope at the pulse point, and pumps air into the cuff until it is inflated and presses tightly around the arm. This pressure cuts off circulation in the artery in the upper arm, forcing its walls together. Because there is no blood flow, no sounds are heard through the stethoscope. As the doctor slowly releases pressure in the cuff, blood begins to flow through the artery.

The doctor listens carefully and notes the gauge reading at two points: when sounds first become audible and when they completely disappear. The first reading, the *systole*, indicates the pressure at which the heart pushes blood through the body (and the pressure at which it leaves the left ventricle). The *diastole*, the second reading, indicates the force arteries exert on the blood as the heart is "resting," or filling with blood between contractions. The upper limit on normal blood pressure for adults is considered to be a systolic of 140 and a diastolic of 90. Blood pressure gauges are usually filled with mercury (like a thermometer) and marked off in millimeters; a blood pressure reading of 120 systolic and 80 diastolic is recorded as 120/80 mm Hg and is read "120 over 80 millimeters of mercury." Though it is normal for blood pressure to rise temporarily during exercise or in response to stress, high blood pressure becomes a problem when it is constant.

Traditionally, doctors were able to listen to the sounds of the heart and lungs by placing their ear close to the patient's chest, a procedure known as auscultation. The original stethoscope—

a rolled tube of paper and a hollow wooden cylinder—was invented in 1819 by René Laënnec. (*Stethos* is the Greek word for "chest.") Though Laënnec's straight stethoscopes look very different from the stethoscopes used today, the concept is still the same: a listening device with one end placed on the patient's chest and the other against the doctor's ear.

Doctors listen to heart sounds at four different places on the patient's chest that correspond to the locations of the four valves. The first sound in the heart's "lub-dub" beat is the shutting of valves between atria and ventricles during systole. The second sound is the shutting of valves between ventricles and arteries as the heart rests and refills at diastole.

Sometimes auscultation results in the discovery of a heart murmur—any extra sound beyond the "lub-dub" of the heartbeat. Some heart murmurs are "innocent"; others point to problems. Causes of heart murmurs include valves that are not functioning properly, abnormal openings in the heart, inflammation of the pericardial sac, which surrounds the heart, and damage from rheumatic fever.

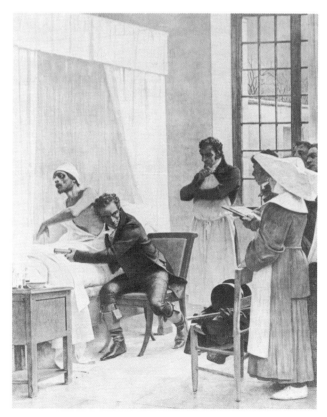

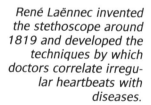

René Laënnec invented the stethoscope around 1819 and developed the techniques by which doctors correlate irregular heartbeats with diseases.

Chest X rays are useful diagnostic tools because certain heart problems—for example, an enlarged chamber or a structural defect—will result in a change in the normal heart silhouette. They are also used to check for problems with the lungs.

More sophisticated techniques are used to pinpoint problems when a heart disorder is suspected. Echocardiography is an ultrasound technique that bounces high-frequency sound waves against the heart; the resultant echoes produce a clear and detailed image of the working heart that doctors view on what looks like a television screen.

The electrical impulses responsible for the heartbeat vary in intensity and direction throughout the cardiac cycle. The *electrocardiograph*, or EKG, measures and records these currents and is a boon in detecting normal and abnormal heartbeats, heart strain, damage, and enlargement. The doctor places pairs of electrodes onto various parts of the body and measures the differences in electrical potential between them. One method uses three pairs of electrodes to give a picture of overall heart activity. One set of electrodes is hooked up to the left and right arm, one to the left and right leg, and the last to the left arm and leg. Several other electrodes are placed on the chest, closer to the

By means of wires attached to the limbs and chest, an electrocardiogram (EKG) measures the flow of electrical current through the heart's muscles before and during muscular contraction.

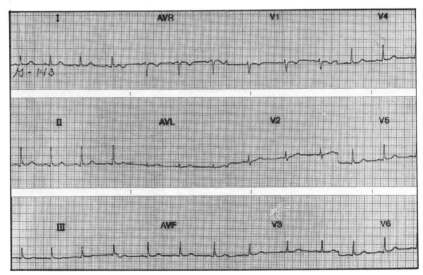

heart, to allow the doctor to pick up minute defects and to help locate the specific sites of any heart problems.

A normally functioning heart will produce a characteristic printout. To analyze the printout, the cardiologist examines the appearance of five waves that indicate the electrical impulses at various points of the cardiac cycle. The P wave indicates the electric impulse generated right before the atria contract. The Q, R, and S waves indicate the electrical impulse that precedes ventricular contraction, and the T wave is the impulse present as the ventricles relax. Heart disorders produce distinctive variations in waveforms. An EKG is a painless procedure and takes only a few minutes. A Holter monitor—developed in 1961 and named for its designer, Dr. Norman Holter—is a mobile EKG device worn by the patient that can monitor heart rate for 24 to 48 hours.

Magnetic resonance imaging, or MRI, is a scanning technique in which the body part under examination is put into a magnetic field and exposed to different levels of radio frequency. Because different particles in the body react uniquely, when the frequency is turned off, variations in energy emitted can be used to create a three-dimensional image.

Invasive Techniques

The first cardiac catheterization was performed by Dr. Werner Forssmann in 1929—on himself. Forssmann wanted to find a method of studying heart function directly and a way to introduce drugs into the circulatory system during emergencies. Practicing on corpses, he became skilled at passing a fine tube into a vein near the elbow and gently pushing it through the vessel until it was near the right side of the heart. Finally, he attempted this on himself and, with the catheter in his heart, walked from his office to another department to have a confirming X ray taken. Nowadays, cardiac catheterization is performed with the patient under local anesthesia. The catheter is treated with a dye impervious to radiation, making its progress visible when the X rays from a fluoroscope are directed on the chest.

Cardiac catheterization is an invaluable diagnostic and treatment tool. It can provide information about the amount of pressure within the heart or across a valve, the presence and quantity of substances present in the blood, how much blood the heart is pumping, and resistance to blood flow in a given area. Photosensitive dye can be injected through the catheter to take pictures of the heart and its vessels and chambers. Without cardiac catheterization, locating the exact site of arterial damage and gaining access to it would be next to impossible.

Angiocardiography uses cardiac-catheter technology to view arteries, veins, or heart chambers. Medical practitioners inject dye through a catheter into the area to be viewed and take a rapid series of X rays of its progress and simultaneously view it on a screen. Blood vessels can be seen in great detail using this technique. Anatomy, diseased areas, and blood flow are also observable. When the dye is injected, it may cause an uncomfortable, but temporary, feeling of heat in the area. When used to view arteries, the technique is called arteriography. *Radionuclide imaging* is another viewing technique that uses radioactive materials administered intravenously to produce images of the heart and circulatory system.

Catheters can also measure pressure gradients in the heart's four chambers; pressure readings are given in millimeters of mercury, like standard blood pressure readings. The right atrium is the recipient of deoxygenated blood from the veins; from a resting state of 0 mm, pressure on this chamber peaks during atrial contraction to about 8 mm. The right ventricle sends blood to the lungs for reoxygenation. From a resting state of about 4 mm, pressure reaches between 15 and 30 mm during ventricular contraction.

Pressure on the left atrium peaks at up to 20 mm when it receives oxygen-rich blood from the lungs; it may reach 16 mm at atrial contraction and dip to below 10 mm when at rest. The left ventricle is subject to up to 140 mm of pressure as it contracts and sends blood to the body; at rest this drops to about 12 mm of pressure. These are normal pressures in the heart. A variety of different heart problems result in unusual pressure gradients, but being able to pinpoint the aberration to a specific part of the cardiac cycle helps diagnose the problem.

•   •   •   •

CHAPTER 2

HISTORICAL BACKGROUND

St. Valentine's Day is a celebration of courtship and love, and the main symbol of amorous feelings has always been the human heart.

Western culture has long considered the heart both a physical and spiritual center. Alone among the body's organs, the heart was deemed sacred—and irreparable if damaged—by doctors and philosophers in times past. Two thousand years ago, the Greek physician Hippocrates believed that all injuries to the heart were necessarily fatal, a common belief for centuries until doctors and scientists gradually learned otherwise.

SURGERY AND SHOCKS

An autopsy report from the early 1600s discusses two cases in which evidence of nonfatal injuries to the heart were found. During the 1820s the French surgeon Baron Dominique-Jean Larrey saved a patient by draining fluid from a stab wound to the heart. And in 1896 a German surgeon, Ludwig Rehn, successfully stitched together a heart wound. One year later, heart massage was successfully used to revive an individual whose heart had stopped beating.

Other doctors looked to electricity as a way to treat heart problems. A new branch of science, electrophysiology, came into being. After noting the effects of inadvertent electrocution on the human body, scientists wondered if electricity in the body was responsible for normal muscle motion. In 1770 an Italian doctor, Louis Galvani, accidentally applied an electrical current to a frog

Ludwig Rehn inaugurated cardiac surgery when, in 1896, he stitched a lacerated heart.

he was preparing for dissection, and the frog's muscles began to contract wildly.

Once word of this discovery spread, electricity began to be seen as a divine, life-giving force, and doctors (and quacks) began to use shock treatment to treat a host of ailments. In 1774 electric shock was successfully used to revive a five-year-old boy in London who had stopped breathing after falling out of a window. Though no one at the time understood why the technique had worked—in fact the child's heart had gone into an abnormal rhythm that electric shock stabilized—a variety of crude electrical devices were designed and used with resuscitation in mind.

In 1856, Rudolph Albert von Kölliker and Heinrich Müller, two Swiss physicians, provided the first evidence that the heart contains an electrical current: A section of nerve and muscle from a frog leg placed on a beating heart twitched with each of the heart's contractions. What electrophysiologists needed now was a way to monitor the heart's newly discovered electrical properties throughout the cardiac cycle. Then, in 1876, the English physician Augustus Waller demonstrated his EKG machine: electrodes linked the patient's body to a capillary electrometer, which measured electrical pressure. Waller's concept was good, but his machine was primitive and inaccurate. The German scientist William Einthoven refined the EKG, and by the century's end an accurate EKG machine existed, for which Einthoven eventually won the 1924 Nobel Prize in physiology and medicine.

THE TWENTIETH CENTURY

Considering that most doctors were still wary of treating the heart at the beginning of the 20th century, no one could have foretold the tremendous diagnostic and treatment breakthroughs in store. The efforts of medics on the battlefields of World War I to surgically repair soldiers' heart wounds helped demystify the heart. The first successful attempt to repair an obstructed heart valve took place in 1925, but it was followed by several failures.

As general surgical techniques improved—including the wide use of anesthesia and the ability to control respiration—more advances in cardiac surgery followed. In 1938, Robert Gross, a surgeon at Harvard Medical School in Boston, successfully cor-

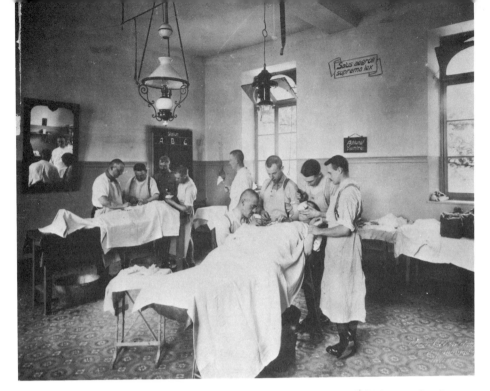

Techniques for heart surgery were advanced in the field hospitals of World War I.

rected a common heart defect called *patent ductus arteriosus*, in which blood leaks from the aorta to the pulmonary artery. The first bypass surgery—creating an alternate route around a blood vessel blockage by linking together other veins or arteries—was performed in 1944 by Dr. Alfred Blalock at Johns Hopkins University.

Both these milestones involved surgery on the heart's surface. To work within the heart required temporarily stopping or controlling heart and lung function while surgery proceeded. One method used in the 1950s borrowed the concept of hibernation, in which an animal "sleeps" through winter as his or her body temperature drops and metabolism slows down. A patient was anesthetized and then cooled down with a cold-water-and-ice bath, special blankets, drugs, or blood-cooling machines. Once surgery was completed, the patient was warmed in a bath or with a special electric blanket. But there were drawbacks to this technique. Temperatures below 30 degrees Fahrenheit tend to make the heart muscles fibrillate, or twitch, which is potentially fatal. Surgery had to be performed very quickly because cooling someone for more than 7 to 10 minutes can permanently damage his or her nervous system.

A heart-lung machine to pump the blood through the body and oxygenate it was sorely needed. One of the first heart-lung machines was developed by John Gibbon, an American professor of surgery, and built with his wife's help. In 1954, Gibbon used his machine during surgery to repair a heart defect. The heart-lung machine had two pumps: one forced blood through the arteries, the other, through an artificial lung, where it picked up oxygen. For 25 minutes, the heart-lung machine completely assumed the patient's normal heart function.

Biological life-support systems were also experimented with. Rather than using machinery to pump and oxygenate blood during surgery, the heart and lung functions of one person could be "married" to those of another in a technique called cross-circulation. A catheter linked one of the patient's veins to one of his or her donor's veins. Blood entered the donor's system where it was pumped and oxygenated. Another catheter linked donor and patient artery to artery so that oxygenated blood returned to the patient's body. From 1955 onward a heart surgeon named Walton Lillehei at the University of Minnesota performed more than 50 operations in this fashion. Cross-circulation eventually proved to be too risky. Donors ran a high risk of infection, and in one case a donor suffered brain damage when an air bubble entered her artery.

Another version of the heart-lung machine was developed by Richard De Wall in the early 1950s. This bubble oxygenator had a chamber in which venous blood was mixed with large oxygen bubbles, de-bubbled (a bubble in the bloodstream can be fatal or, as mentioned above, cause serious damage), and then was pumped back into an artery. Though this was an effective way of oxygenating blood for short surgeries, direct, repeated exposure of blood to the gas mixture ultimately damages blood cells. Scientists developed another procedure using membrane oxygenators to imitate the way carbon dioxide and oxygen are exchanged in blood circulated through the lungs. A thin plastic membrane is placed between the blood and the oxygen, thus permitting oxygenation but preventing damage to the blood. Both types of heart-lung machines are currently in use; doctors usually use membrane oxygenators for longer surgeries.

THE ELECTRIC HEART

While heart surgery was in its infancy, scientists were gaining ground in the field of electrophysiology. Sir Thomas Lewis spent the years 1915 to 1925 taking electrocardiograms and documenting fluctuations in heart rhythms. It became clear that heart problems such as chest pain and shortness of breath frequently result from arrhythmias, irregularities in heartbeat caused by disturbances in the heart's electrical signaling system.

There followed a resurgence of interest in the old records of electrical resuscitation efforts. Was there a way to use electrical current to stabilize an arrhythmic heart? In the 1920s, Drs. J. L. Prevost and F. Battelli hooked up frogs to EKG machines and observed their heart rhythms as they were electrocuted. When the EKG showed an arrhythmia, the researchers applied a second jolt of electricity. And after trial and error they determined the exact moment when an electric shock could halt the abnormal rhythm. This process of *defibrillation* worked on frogs, but 20 years would pass before it was attempted on humans.

Meanwhile, it became clear that as useful as the EKG was, it was still almost impossible to determine the exact source and location of an arrhythmia from outside the heart. Dr. Werner Forssmann, the father of cardiac catheterization, attempted to record electrical impulses from inside the heart. He was able to pick up sounds but could not distinguish cardiac signals from other background noise. A few years later, other cardiologists were better able to retrieve cardiac signals, and by the mid-1950s clear, precise *intracardiac* (within-the-heart) recordings were easily produced. These recordings pinpoint the exact location of arrhythmias.

A milestone in electrophysiologic medicine was reached in 1947 when Dr. Claude Beck, a cardiac surgeon at Case Western Reserve Hospital, used a defibrillator to resuscitate a 14-year-old patient who had gone into arrhythmia during surgery. It was a stroke of luck that the device, still used only during animal experiments, was even present in the operating room. The use of a defibrillator is now standard practice in treating a heart that has stopped or is dangerously arrhythmic.

SPARE PARTS

The 1950s and 1960s ushered in the era of replacing dysfunctional parts of the heart and the entire heart itself. The first artificial-valve surgery, using an industrial ball-type valve, was performed in 1953 by Dr. Charles A. Hufnagle. Other valves were designed, and a variety are available on the market today. Biologic heart valves from human and pig donors and valves fashioned from calf-heart pericardium came into use some years later. They work well but do not last as long as artificial valves.

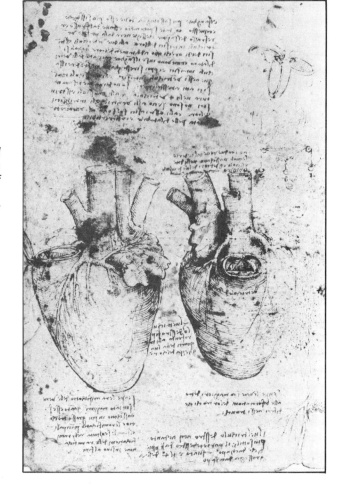

Painter, sculptor, and engineer Leonardo da Vinci, a major figure of the Italian Renaissance, was also fascinated by the human body.

"Biologics," as they are called, are processed before implantation to decrease the chance of their rejection. Artificial valves are made of sterile materials and are more reliable and long lasting. Anticoagulant medicine is essential for people with artificial valves, however, because blood clots readily form around artificial materials.

Strides in *immunosuppressive therapy* during the 1960s meant that the day of the first heart transplant was not far off. Immunosuppressive drugs prevent the immune system from reacting to and rejecting foreign (donated) organs. The first heart transplant was performed by Dr. Christiaan Barnard at Groote Schuur Hospital in Cape Town, South Africa, in 1967. The recipient, Louis Washkansky, died 18 days later of postsurgical infection and organ rejection. One month later, Barnard performed the same operation on Philip Blaiberg, who survived 593 days. Other heart transplants were performed, and survival time increased. Earlier diagnosis of organ rejection, more effective antirejection drugs, and more accurate matching between donor and recipient now mean that 85% of transplant patients survive for one year or more.

Pacemakers

Electronic pacemakers have meant the difference between life and death for people whose hearts beat too irregularly or infrequently to circulate blood through their bodies. In the 1960s, the first pacemakers ran on mercury batteries, which required replacement every two years. Lithium batteries, which now power pacemakers, last for up to 10 years.

A new variety of implantable machine—the *automatic implantable cardioverter defibrillator* (AICD)—senses aberrant heart rhythms and then shocks the heart to restore normal rhythms. The AICD is a lifesaver for anyone with arrhythmia who does not respond to medication. Its designers, Drs. Michael Mirowski and Morton Mower of Baltimore's Sinai Hospital, first implanted the device in a human in 1980. The AICD was approved by the Food and Drug Administration (FDA) for general use in 1985.

A permanent artificial heart is still an experimental undertaking, though mechanical hearts are used on a temporary basis to tide over transplant patients waiting for donor hearts. On De-

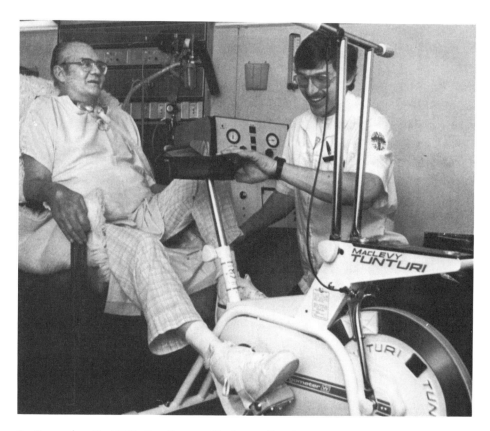

On December 2, 1982, Dr. Barney Clark was fitted with a permanent artificial heart to relieve a serious case of congestive heart disease. The device kept him alive for 112 days before a host of complications proved fatal.

cember 2, 1982, Dr. Barney Clark became the first recipient of the permanent artificial heart. At 61, Dr. Clark was too old for a biological heart transplant, and medication had been unsuccessful in treating his heart failure. The Jarvik-7 heart was designed by Dr. Robert Jarvik at the Division of Artificial Organs in Salt Lake City and implanted by Dr. William DeVries and his team at the Utah University College of Medicine. Although the heart itself is implantable, the recipient is tethered by a hose to an air compressor, which provides pumping power. Dr. Clark lived for 112 difficult days after implantation, suffering seizures, kidney failure, lung problems, and other disorders. The difficulties experienced by Clark and the few other recipients of permanent artificial hearts led the FDA to open an investigation into the use of these devices in 1985. Initially, the FDA permitted "investigative use" of the heart, which limited its implantation to situations that the agency could monitor. In January 1990, the FDA withdrew its approval of the artificial heart's use altogether, citing life-endangering deficiencies in the procedures used to manufacture the hearts. These artificial hearts are still being used overseas, with some success, and once the FDA's complaints have been addressed, it is more than likely that American use will resume.

•   •   •   •

CHAPTER 3

CONGENITAL
HEART
DEFECTS

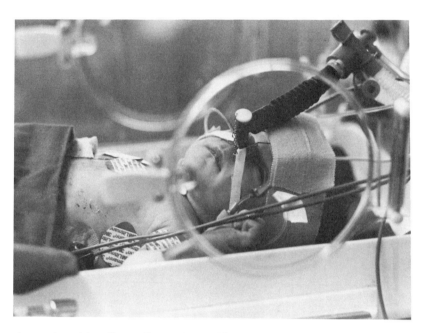

Eleven-day-old Hollie Roffery, pictured here in 1984 at the National Heart Hospital in London, England, was at that time the youngest heart transplant patient in medical history.

Congenital heart defects are abnormalities that afflict the heart at birth. Cardiac defects are among the most common birth defects and occur in 1 out of every 120 live births. Causes are not always clear; a defect in the baby's chromosomes, illness in the pregnant mother, or prenatal exposure to radiation, alcohol, or certain drugs may lead to physical problems in the infant.

Ultrasound can be used during pregnancy to detect congenital problems and allows parents and doctors time to plan treatment before the infant is born. The outlook for a child born with a congenital defect is much brighter now than in the past.

A heart murmur is one clue to the presence of a heart defect in a newborn baby. Or, instead of a healthy ruddiness, the baby might be cyanotic—have a bluish tinge to its skin. Noninvasive tests give the doctor a better idea of the condition of the child's heart. Defects in the heart's size and shape can be seen in a chest X ray, and an EKG reveals different areas of the heart and how well they are working. An echocardiogram provides a clear and detailed image of the infant's heart. Cardiac catheterization might also be performed to run a variety of diagnostic tests, including checking oxygen levels in the heart's blood and measuring pressure across the valves. Generally, structural defects in the heart weaken it and create a higher risk of infection—antibiotics are often given to prevent infections.

SEPTAL DEFECTS

Septal defects are gaps in the septum that permit blood to flow between the right and left sides of the heart. If the hole lies in the section of the septum between the two atria, it is an *atrial septal defect*. A *ventricular septal defect* is an opening between the two lower chambers, the ventricles. Babies with septal defects are often cyanotic at birth, and characteristic heart murmurs are audible.

Ventricular septal defects are generally no bigger than a half inch across, whereas openings in the atria can be up to one inch across. The left side of the heart is naturally subject to higher pressure than the right, so if there is a hole between the ventricles, blood will flow from the left side toward the right side. The right ventricle pumps more blood than usual to the lungs. After a time, the lungs become damaged and flooded with extra blood and resist the entry of new blood for oxygenation. Now the direction of blood flow through the hole in the septum is reversed from right to left, and unoxygenated blood is pumped from the left ventricle through the body.

The same sequence of events occurs with atrial septal defects: Blood flows from the left side of the heart to the right, pulmonary circulation is overstressed, and the direction of blood flow reverses itself. Although the condition is initially less severe, the same set of symptoms as those described for the ventricular septal defect may set in later. Both septal defects, if untreated, will lead to heart failure. Stress on the heart from the abnormal bloodflow pattern will show up in an EKG, an X ray will show heart enlargement, and echocardiography will reveal a septal defect.

Heart failure is treated with digitalis, diuretics, and salt restriction. Afflicted infants usually respond well to treatment with drugs. If these measures are not effective, the infant's septum may require surgical repair.

In a condition called *patent ductus arteriosus*, blood flows unchecked from the aorta to the pulmonary artery through an open passageway, sending nourishment intended for the entire body just to the lungs. This passage is ordinarily open before birth, but normally closes itself off within several hours after an infant is born. As might be expected, its failure to do so is more common in premature than in full-term babies. A heart murmur is the usual tip-off, but abnormal EKG results, X rays, and heart contractions also point to this defect. If the duct remains open, a drug called indomethacin may be used to constrict it, or surgery can be used to close it.

CYANOTIC DEFECTS

Congenital cyanotic heart disorders are those in which structural defects cause deoxygenated blood to be pumped throughout the body. Babies with this disorder have bluish skin, hence the term "blue babies." *Transposition of the great arteries* and *tetralogy of Fallot* are two examples of cardiac cyanotic defects.

In transposition of the great arteries, the aorta and the pulmonary arteries have reversed positions, and an abnormal opening between the right and left sides of the heart is also present. Since the aorta is wrongly connected to the right ventricle, it circulates deoxygenated blood through the body. Moreover, the pulmonary artery, which is connected to the left ventricle, sends already-oxygenated blood back to the lungs again.

Babies born with this condition have normal EKGs, but X rays will reveal the arterial transposition. Either echocardiography or cardiac catheterization is used to confirm the diagnosis. Drugs are sometimes given to help increase blood flow in and out of the lungs, which results in a greater volume of oxygenated blood. The opening in the septum might also be temporarily widened to permit oxygenated blood to flow into the right side of the heart so that it can be circulated by the transposed aorta. Surgical repair—which usually transposes the positions of the pulmonary vein and the superior vena cava to correct blood flow—is performed as soon as possible.

Tetralogy of Fallot—first described by Étienne-Louis Arthur Fallot in 1880—is a complex defect with four characteristic features. A large hole in the septum permits blood to flow back and forth between the right and left ventricles. The aorta is incorrectly positioned over the ventricular septal defect, so unoxygenated blood enters the aorta for circulation. The pulmonary valve is narrowed, which reduces blood flow from the right heart to the lungs. And from trying to compensate for the narrowed pulmonary valve, the right ventricle becomes more muscular and enlarged than usual.

The condition's severity depends on the extent to which the pulmonary valve's function is compromised. If enough blood reaches the lungs for oxygenation, the infant may not even be cyanotic. But if the pulmonary valve is almost completely occluded or closed up, the infant will suffer convulsions, periods of unconsciousness, and infections. Oxygen supplementation and morphine are commonly administered to ease symptoms, and as soon as possible, corrective surgery is performed to close the hole in the septum and open the pulmonary valve.

BLOOD-FLOW OBSTRUCTIONS

Blood flow to the heart can be obstructed for a variety of reasons, including *coarctation of the aorta* and *pulmonary valve* and *aortic valve stenosis*. (*Stenosis* means "narrowing.") Coarctation of the aorta, in which a section of the aorta is narrowed or pinched, compromises blood flow to the lower part of the body. In infants, a severe closure of the aorta might lead to heart failure. Drugs are given to dilate the duct, and supplementary oxygen is administered to help breathing. Once blood flow resumes, surgery to repair the defect can be performed.

In older children, coarctation of the aorta results in highly varied blood pressure and pulse readings throughout the body, with higher readings in the upper extremities. A sound called a *bruit* is often audible through a stethoscope placed directly over the defect. The coarctation is often visible in an X ray. The left ventricle may show signs of overwork in an EKG. Surgery to remove or bypass the damaged section of the aorta can be performed in cases in which blood pressure in the upper extremities is extreme or heart failure occurs.

In pulmonary valve stenosis the pulmonary valve is narrower than usual, and the right ventricle—which is linked to the lungs via the pulmonary valve—has to pump harder to make up for this defect. In newborn infants this is an emergency situation because blood cannot reach the lungs for oxygenation. The infant is usually cyanotic; EKG, X ray, echocardiography, and cardiac catheterization may all be used to determine the extent to which the right ventricle's function is being compromised. Drugs are used to keep the valve as open as possible, and an artificial shunt is created to maintain blood flow between the right ventricle and lungs. Surgery to repair the valve may be performed repeatedly through childhood.

In preschoolers, a heart murmur is the first sign of this defect. An EKG will show that the right ventricle is overworked, and a cardiac catheter is used to measure the amount of pressure in this chamber. A reading of over 60 mm Hg warrants surgery.

When the aortic valve is narrowed, as in aortic stenosis, it hampers the left ventricle's effort to get blood through to the aorta and the rest of the body. In an infant, a narrowed aortic valve is difficult to detect. If the left ventricle appears not to be functioning well, an EKG will indicate less than adequate circulation and cardiac output. Surgery is usually performed to improve the valve's function, and when the child is older, the aortic valve itself can be replaced with a biologic or synthetic valve.

In older children, aortic stenosis is signaled by a heart murmur. EKG and X ray are employed first; if there is evidence of blockage, invasive techniques like cardiac catheterization follow. If the valve performs adequately, the child is regularly monitored, but the condition is left untreated. When the left ventricle shows

definite signs of dysfunction, surgical treatment may be necessary to enlarge the valve's opening. Valve replacement may eventually be necessary.

Rarely, an infant will be born with an incompletely formed—
or *hypoplastic*—heart. In a rare and serious malformation called
hypoplastic left heart syndrome, the left side of the heart is under-
developed. This defect used to be accepted as incurable and fatal,
but a complex two-operation procedure has a 44% success rate
in rebuilding a functional heart.

An unborn child can survive in the womb with these defects
because its mother's circulatory system works for them both. It
is only when the baby is born and must rely on its own circulatory
system that many of these defects become apparent and cause
problems.

MARFAN'S SYNDROME

Marfan's syndrome is an inherited disorder resulting in a range
of connective tissue abnormalities that include cardiac problems.
It is a progressive disease with a poor prognosis; the average age
of death for persons with Marfan's syndrome is 32. More than
90% of Marfan's deaths result from cardiovascular problems. The
disorder is difficult to diagnose because it usually occurs without
symptoms and there are no specific tests to confirm its presence.

Individuals with Marfan's are unusually tall and thin, with an
arm span greater than their height. Someone with Marfan's generally suffers from one of many cardiac defects, including a pro-
lapsed mitral valve, an atrial septal defect, mitral regurgitation,
and a pulmonary or aortic *aneurysm* (a balloonlike bulge in the
arterial wall). The deformed and weakened sections of the heart
are vulnerable to bacteria in the bloodstream; thus bacterial endocarditis may also set in. The various heart defects someone
with Marfan's may have can be temporarily corrected. But because damaged tissues continue to disintegrate, the long-term
benefits of surgery are of questionable value.

•   •   •   •

CHAPTER 4
· · · · · · · · · · · · · · · · ·
INFECTIOUS
CARDIOVASCULAR
DISORDERS

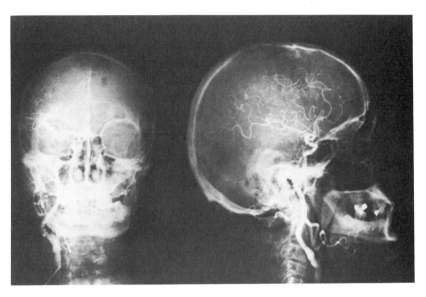

The malformed blood vessels appearing in this X ray show the effects of a stroke.

Although high blood pressure, coronary heart disease (CHD), and stroke are the most common cardiovascular problems in the United States, elsewhere in the world the most common heart problems for both adults and children are valve disorders, which are often caused by rheumatic heart disease. This difference can be attributed to discrepancies in general health, and diet especially, between developed and undeveloped countries. Valves may also be damaged by bacterial and viral infections, congenital disorders, or a heart attack. Dysfunctional valves force the heart to work harder to maintain normal blood flow; in addition, any weakened section of the heart, including a malfunctioning valve, is prone to infection.

RHEUMATIC HEART DISEASE

Rheumatic heart disease is one lethal side effect from a bout of untreated rheumatic fever, which in turn results from a streptococcal (bacterial) infection. Rheumatic fever is an inflammatory disease that targets connective tissue in the heart, skin, brain, and joints.

Most cases of rheumatic fever in the United States occur in school-age children and are the result of an untreated strep throat. Symptoms include a sore throat, fever, swollen neck and jaw glands, headache, nausea, and vomiting. A throat culture may detect the streptococcus bacteria, and antibiotics are prescribed to cure the infection. It is very easy to diagnose and treat strep throat, and doing so prevents progression of the infection to rheumatic fever.

There are no specific tests for rheumatic fever. Its symptoms include fever that lasts several days, body and joint pain, a rash, poor appetite, and *chorea*—involuntary and spasmodic muscle movements of the face and limbs.

The doctor makes a diagnosis of rheumatic fever from a variety of indirect evidence, including fever, evidence of a strep infection, and an elevated white blood cell count (a sign that the body is reacting to an infection). X rays and an EKG are taken to check for heart damage. If valvular damage has already occurred, the patient may be cyanotic or have a heart murmur. In advanced cases, doctors may perform cardiac catheterization, angiocardiography, and echocardiography to pinpoint the location and type of damage. Antibiotics are given to combat the infection, and other treatment follows, depending on the extent of damage to the heart and valves.

After several decades of declining incidence, the mid-1980s showed an increase in the number of rheumatic fever cases in the United States. One to two percent of schoolchildren in this country show signs of rheumatic heart disease.

BACTERIAL ENDOCARDITIS

Bacterial endocarditis is a severe infection of the tissues lining the heart and the heart valves. At risk for infection are individuals with artificial valves, those who have had surgery on their vascular systems, those with heart deformities, and intravenous drug users (shooting up with contaminated needles introduces bacteria into the body).

Bacterial endocarditis occurs when bacteria in the bloodstream attack a heart valve or any weakened, deformed section of the heart. When bacterial growth sets in, disturbing the heart valve's operations, potentially hazardous blood clots, aneurysms, and abscesses may form in the heart. The physical damage bacterial endocarditis inflicts is permanent, and the bacteria themselves may migrate to other parts of the body, especially the kidneys where, if they are allowed to remain untreated, heart or kidney failure—and even death—may result.

Fever, night sweats, and fatigue are common symptoms. A blood culture test will reveal the bacteria's presence, and a heart murmur related to the infection may be present. High doses of antibiotics are often needed to treat the condition, and sometimes surgery to correct damage to the body and remove infected areas may be performed. People at risk for bacterial endocarditis are generally put on a preventive course of antibiotics before and after they undergo dental or surgical work that may introduce bacteria into the bloodstream.

PERICARDITIS

Infection and inflammation or other disorders of the pericardium, the sac that surrounds the heart, are called pericarditis. Rheumatic fever, arthritis, heart attack, pericardial injury or tumor, and endocarditis may all cause pericarditis. Pain, especially upon breathing, a dry cough, and fever are common symptoms. Sometimes the pericardial layers become so inflamed they cannot slide over each other in their normal fashion, which in turn creates a sound that is audible through a stethoscope. An EKG will show abnormalities. Painkillers and anti-inflammatory drugs are prescribed, as are medications to treat any infection that may be present.

In chronic cases of pericarditis, the pericardium may become permanently hardened and inflexible, and the tissue damage and infection may cause the space between the two layers to close. Further tissue damage and scarring may form a tight layer around the heart, a condition called *constrictive pericarditis*. If the pericardium impedes heart function, it may be surgically removed. Another pericardial condition involves the accumulation of excess fluid between the layers, forming a *pericardial effusion*, which also exerts undue pressure on the heart. Excess fluid may be drained from the pericardial sac; in less advanced cases, sodium reduction, rest, and diuretics are successful treatments. A chest X ray will show abnormalities in the heart's silhouette, and echocardiography will reveal fluid accumulation, if present.

KAWASAKI DISEASE

Kawasaki disease, the cause of which is unknown, usually affects children under five years old. Although scientists believe Kawasaki disease is caused by a virus, the condition does not seem to be contagious. Symptoms include swollen lymph glands in the neck, inflamed mouth, lips, and throat, and irritated eyes. The child also runs a fever and may have a body rash and swollen feet and hands.

No specific treatment exists for Kawasaki disease. Aspirin is given to reduce fever and inflammation and keep blood clots from forming. Intravenous administration of gamma globulin—which contains antibodies that help fight infections—has been effective in preventing the disease from damaging the heart.

In 20% of cases of Kawasaki disease, heart muscle or coronary arteries are damaged. Aneurysms may develop, and sometimes a blood clot will form at the site and block the artery. *Myocarditis* (inflammation of the heart muscle) or pericarditis may set in. The heart valves may also be affected, and the heartbeat may alter. Sometimes these problems are only temporary. An EKG will detect changes in the heart's rhythm or damage to the heart muscle itself, and echocardiograms will indicate damage to the arteries.

VALVULAR HEART DISEASE

Heart damage caused by rheumatic fever and other infections typically involves *valvular insufficiency*, in which valves cannot completely close, thus allowing blood to flow backward through them, and valvular stenosis, in which valves cannot fully open and thus impede the flow of blood. Other causes of damage to the valves include abnormal tissue growths, calcium deposits, heart attack, and the process of aging.

Valvular damage forces the heart to work harder to maintain a smooth forward flow of blood, overexertion that, because the heart is a muscular organ, causes it to enlarge, in turn making it less efficient. Because the left side of the heart is responsible for systemic circulation, damage to the mitral and/or aortic valves will have serious consequences. Disorders of the pulmonary valve are usually congenital. Once a valve is damaged, it may either be surgically repaired or replaced. Doctors prefer to repair faulty valves in infants and children—there are no good artificial valves for very young and still-growing children. *Balloon valvuloplasty*, or dilation of a valve's opening using a balloon passed through a catheter, is another way of treating narrowed or blocked valves.

MITRAL VALVE DISORDERS

The mitral valve lies between the left atrium and left ventricle. It directs a steady supply of blood to the left ventricle, the pumping chamber for blood meant to nourish the body. Variations in the shape of the valve sometimes prevent its cusps from forming a complete seal. This condition is known as *mitral valve prolapse*. Other causes of insufficiency include soft-tissue tumors on the valve, rheumatic fever, Marfan's syndrome, and atrial septal defects. Many people do not even realize their mitral valve leaks because mild cases are symptomless.

In more dysfunctional mitral valves, backflow and continual leakage of blood result in irregular heartbeat, chest pain, fatigue, headache, and shortness of breath. Heart palpitations and murmurs are readily heard during a doctor's exam. Chest X rays will show enlargement of the left ventricle. The echocardiogram provides more details about the left ventricle's ability to function. An EKG may show atrial fibrillation, or rapid contraction, in the left atrium as that chamber struggles to function with excess blood.

In cases in which infection has caused mitral regurgitation the patient is put on a regimen of antibiotics. Anticoagulant drugs are prescribed to prevent clots from forming in the left atrium's slow-moving blood. Drugs are used to slow the heart rate and reduce stress on the heart. Since adequate blood circulation is difficult to maintain with a faulty mitral valve, the latter can be replaced with an animal valve or a man-made substitute.

Mitral valve stenosis results in an obstruction of blood flow between the left atrium and left ventricle and ultimately puts extra pressure on the lungs and right ventricle to push blood into the left atrium. In adults, mitral valve stenosis is almost always caused by rheumatic fever. In infants, where the condition is caused only congenitally, the lungs are particularly susceptible to damage, and mitral valve stenosis may be fatal.

Someone with a very mild case of mitral valve stenosis can

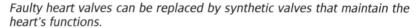
Faulty heart valves can be replaced by synthetic valves that maintain the heart's functions.

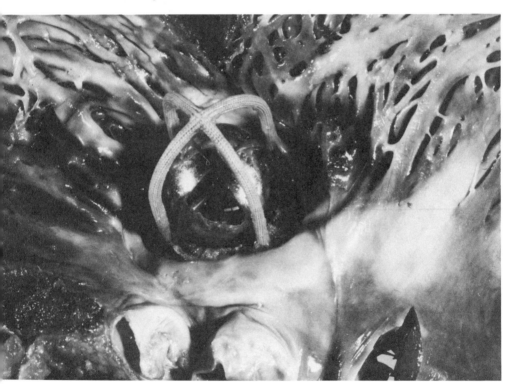

remain symptom-free for many years. Then fatigue or shortness of breath upon exertion may become noticeable as the amount of blood and oxygen leaving the left ventricle progressively declines. Fluid begins to collect in the lungs, and blood pools in the left atrium, where it tends to form clots.

Heart murmurs will be audible, an EKG will show signs of left atrium overload, and an X ray will reveal changes in the heart's silhouette. An echocardiogram will provide information about the size of the left atrium and the exact condition of the valve. Cardiac catheterization is used to obtain pressure readings for the left atrium.

Drugs are used to slow down the heart rate and reduce pressure and stress on the heart. If the left atrium has begun to fibrillate, beating more rapidly than usual in its efforts to deal with the extra blood, a drug such as digitalis is used to increase the strength and effectiveness of the heart's contractions. Anticoagulants are prescribed to prevent the pooled left atrium blood from forming clots. When the condition is so severe that an individual shows symptoms even when at rest, the valve is surgically dilated, fused sections are separated, or the entire valve is replaced. Replacement surgery is usually successful; 70% to 85% of patients survive at least 5 years.

AORTIC VALVE DISORDERS

The aortic valve conducts oxygenated blood to the aorta for distribution throughout the body. When it is damaged, the aortic valve can almost never be repaired, but doctors can now replace the entire valve, and this procedure has a 5-year survival rate of 85%.

Aortic insufficiency causes the backward flow of blood from the aorta into the left ventricle. Severe cases in adults are usually due to infection and rheumatic heart disease, whereas mild cases are due to long-term effects of hypertension. Aortic insufficiency in children is generally caused by a structural, congenital defect.

To accommodate extra blood volume, the left ventricle increases its capacity and the amount of blood it pumps. This condition can be tolerated for years and may even be symptomless, but shortness of breath eventually develops. Systolic blood pressure will be unusually high because of the extra force the left ventricle uses to pump out an increased blood volume, but diastolic pressure will be normal. A heart murmur is usually audible. Untreated, aortic backflow can lead to heart failure. Doctors will usually prescribe digitalis to help the heart pump and vasodilators to dilate the arteries; if this is ineffective, they will often replace the aortic valve.

Aortic valve stenosis is the narrowing of the area above, below, and including the aortic valve. The reduction in blood flow from the valve into the aorta for circulation throughout the body is a serious problem. In younger individuals, aortic valve stenosis is usually a congenital defect. In those older than 60, hardening of the valve is due to tissue growth.

Shortness of breath, chest pain, and faintness are typical symptoms. Depending on the severity of the condition and the specific site of narrowing, a variety of abnormal pulses and murmurs can be detected. The left ventricle might be enlarged. Echocardiograms and X rays might show damage to the valve as well as left ventricle enlargement. An abnormal EKG is commonly found. A patient with chest pain (a signal of other heart problems) should undergo coronary angiography to check the condition of the coronary arteries. Valve replacement is often performed.

TRICUSPID VALVE

The tricuspid valve lies between the right atrium and ventricle on the path that leads blood into the lungs for oxygenation. Unusual pressure and dilation of the right ventricle contribute to *tricuspid insufficiency*, causing the backward flow of blood from the right ventricle to the right atrium. Damaged arteries and arterioles in the lungs may reduce the amount of blood the lungs can handle, and this adversely affects the function of the right ventricle. Infection may also prevent the valve from working properly, and sometimes the valve itself is malformed.

Depending on the condition's severity, an EKG will detect right ventricle overload. An unusually pronounced pulse at the neck also indicates the backflow of blood, and X rays will show an enlarged right ventricle. Cardiac catheterization may be used to measure the blood pressure in the right ventricle directly, and angiography is useful in determining if the valve itself is malformed or if the condition is due to problems in the lungs. Tricuspid regurgitation usually requires treatment only if it is caused by an ongoing bacterial infection. Antibiotics are given, and the infected valve is removed and replaced.

Tricuspid stenosis reduces blood flow from the right atrium to the right ventricle. The right atrium distends with excess blood. Fatigue is common because inadequate amounts of blood are being oxygenated. An EKG will show signs of right atrium overload; a chest X ray, right atrium and superior vena cava enlargement. Echocardiography will also indicate an enlarged right atrium. Rarely is the condition severe enough to warrant valve surgery or replacement.

CONGESTIVE HEART FAILURE

If left untreated, valve disorders lead to congestive heart failure, a condition that occurs after repeated damage to the heart. Over time, cardiac output decreases and fails to satisfy the body tissues' demands for oxygen and nutrients. Blood backs up in these tissues, and fluid begins to collect throughout the body—a condition known as *edema*—typically in the legs and ankles and in the lungs, where it complicates the process of breathing.

There are two important components in the development of congestive heart failure: underlying and precipitating causes. Among the former are all the diseases mentioned in this chapter, as well as stroke and heart attack, atherosclerosis, high blood pressure, or congenital heart defects, all of which can contribute to structural abnormalities in the heart over a long period of time. But these in themselves are not enough to induce heart failure. Often there is some additional burden on the heart that acts as a precipitating cause. These include pulmonary embolisms, obstructions of blood vessels caused by clots or air bubbles, which elevate pressure in the pulmonary arteries and thus may cause the right ventricle to distend and fail altogether. Arrhythmias are another cause. This disturbance in turn interrupts the contractions of the ventricle. And overeating, too much exercise, and even environmental pressures such as bad weather can disturb cardiac performance to the point of heart failure. Medications used to treat congestive heart failure include vasodilators to distend blood vessels and lower blood pressure, making the heart's job easier. Diuretics eliminate extra body fluid, and digitalis helps the heart pump. Rest and a healthful diet also ease symptoms. Treating other complicating factors like high blood pressure or faulty valves also improves heart function.

•   •   •   •

CHAPTER 5
• • • • • • • • • • • • • • •
HYPERTENSION
AND
HEART DISEASE

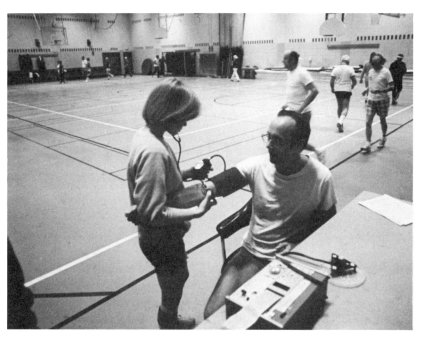

Checking blood pressure is one important way to monitor cardiac health.

Hypertension is another name for chronic high blood pressure and the conditions associated with that disorder. Because high blood pressure not only strains the heart and arteries but also threatens a patient's general well-being, often causing kidney failure and stroke, it is one of the most complex and difficult diseases a physician treats. It is also one of the most prevalent. According to the American Heart Association's estimates for 1987, almost 61 million American adults and children suffer from high blood pressure. In the same year, hypertension claimed the lives of more than 30,000 people in the United States. It is the most widespread cardiovascular disorder—more than 90% of people with heart and blood vessel problems are hypertensive—and for reasons still unknown, blacks in the United States are almost twice as likely as whites to develop this condition.

To make matters worse, high blood pressure often occurs without any symptoms to signal it—many people are not even aware they are suffering from the disorder—making early diagnosis and treatment that much more difficult.

THE HEART, KIDNEYS, AND ARTERIES

The brain and nervous system are responsible, by means of instructions sent throughout the nervous system, for regulating the force with which the heart and arteries push blood through the body. Blood pressure receptors in the carotid arteries and aorta—called *bioreceptors*—signal the brain whenever blood pressure is too high or low.

A variety of substances in the body affect blood pressure. Commonly, the nervous system sends a message to increase blood pressure. A chemical called *norepinephrine* is released when the instructions sent by the central nervous system reach their destination, where *receptors* there respond to the norepinephrine and carry out the instruction.

If the heart is the target organ, it will respond by circulating blood through the body with more force and at a faster rate, resulting in increased blood pressure. The kidneys affect blood pressure by controlling levels of body fluid. If the kidneys are the target organ, they will respond by retaining salt and water, thereby raising the body's fluid levels. Excess salt and water are stored in the body's tissues, which stiffens them and makes it harder for blood to circulate. The heart and arteries have to work harder to force blood through, so blood pressure increases.

Healthy arteries are elastic and contract and dilate with ease. When the arteries receive instructions to raise blood pressure, muscles in the arterial walls contract and cause narrowing of the vessels. The arteries' increased resistance forces the heart to work harder to get blood through them, and blood pressure increases.

The nervous system is not the only controlling factor in determining blood pressure. The heart, kidneys, and arteries also work independently to do the same thing. If someone consumes a great deal of salt, excess fluid will accumulate and circulate in the body. The heart responds by working harder to pump the extra fluid through the system.

The kidneys control blood pressure by producing a hormone called *renin*. When blood flow to one or both kidneys is reduced, the kidneys respond by increasing renin production, which triggers the two adrenal glands (one atop each kidney) to secrete another hormone, *aldosterone*. Aldosterone commands the kidneys to retain sodium. This results in increased fluid in the body, putting pressure on the heart to work harder; this action in turn provides the kidneys with more blood.

CAUSES

It is usually difficult to determine the exact cause of a high-blood-pressure condition, but what is known about how the body regulates the blood pressure system of heart, kidneys, and arteries makes it possible to treat the condition—called *essential* or *primary hypertension*—regardless of its specific cause.

Several factors are implicated for their role in hypertension. Being more than 20% overweight and eating a high-sodium, high-fat diet can create hypertension, and heredity may predispose one to the condition. Age also has a role, for as people grow older, they are generally more likely to develop hypertension, because arteries naturally become somewhat less flexible. Other details of an individual's life-style may also increase the risk of hypertension, including cigarette smoking, alcohol consumption, and stress.

Ten percent of hypertension cases are considered *secondary hypertension*; that is, a kidney problem, tumor, or inborn heart defect causes the disorder. Kidney disorders are suspected if certain blood chemical levels are high. A variety of kidney-function tests can be performed to help determine if problems with either one or both kidneys are causing hypertension. If blockage or narrowed arteries are causing high blood pressure—a condition called *renal artery stenosis*—surgery can be performed to unblock or remove the damaged section. A procedure called *percutaneous transluminal angioplasty* may rule out the need for surgery al-

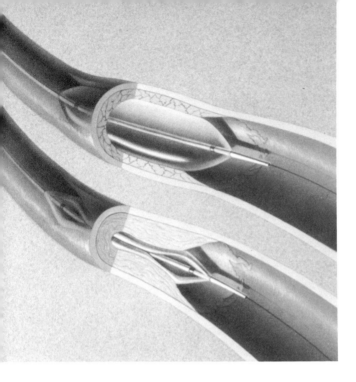

The balloon catheter is inserted into an artery and then inflated, crushing any built-up plaque and widening the passageway.

together. A catheter is advanced into the narrowed artery, and a tiny balloon is guided through it. Inflating the balloon helps widen the artery.

Other causes of secondary hypertension are disorders of the adrenal glands. In *aldosteronism*, an adrenal gland tumor or inflammation causes too much of the hormone aldosterone to be secreted. Removing a tumor, if one is present, or administering diuretics will control the condition. *Pheochromocytoma*, also caused by tumorous growths on the adrenals, results in the release of other hormones (epinephrine and norepinephrine) that raise blood pressure. Surgery to remove the tumors will solve the problem. Sometimes the pituitary gland will overstimulate the adrenals to produce too much of the hormone cortisol. In this disorder, called *Cushing's syndrome*, either gland may need to be removed and hormone replacement therapy given as a follow-up.

Coarctation of the aorta is another organic source of hypertension in which a narrower than usual section of the aorta forces the heart to work harder to pump blood. The doctor can hear this condition when doing a chest exam; it is also indicated by a heart murmur or if blood pressure is high in the arms but low in the legs. A chest X ray or EKG can reveal abnormalities that are present with the condition. Surgery is the usual method by which the narrowed section is repaired.

Hypertension affects the body in several ways. If left untreated, high blood pressure can lead to heart disease, kidney failure, or stroke. It can damage the circulatory system and puts undue stress on the heart. Over time, high blood pressure can also damage arterial walls. Usually smooth and supple, the arteries' inner lining becomes roughened until it is worn away, exposing underlying tissue. Blood cells get caught on the roughened walls and stick to them. As blood cells accumulate, they clog the artery and may cause a blood clot. A blood clot in a coronary artery may lead to a heart attack, and a stroke may occur if a blood clot forms in an artery supplying the brain with blood. If pressure builds up in a clogged artery, it might burst and hemorrhage, also leading to heart attack or stroke.

Because high blood pressure weakens the arteries, it makes them more susceptible to *arteriosclerosis* (*sclerosis* derives from the Greek word for "hardness"), the thickening and hardening of the arteries. A particular type of arteriosclerosis called *atherosclerosis* (*athero*, from the Greek word for "paste") is also common. In this condition, fatty substances, cholesterol, cellular waste, calcium, clotting material in the blood, and other substances combine to form a substance called *plaque* that clogs the artery.

In its efforts to handle increased blood pressure, the heart works harder and gradually enlarges. If hypertension remains untreated, the heart may reach a point where it no longer pumps efficiently. Fluid collects in the lungs and body tissues, and congestive heart failure results.

Kidney damage not only causes hypertension but may also be the result of hypertension. Over time, high blood pressure stiffens and damages arteries and arterioles in the kidneys, making them less able to carry out their job of filtering and purifying blood.

TREATING HYPERTENSION

If an individual's blood pressure is above 200/105, the doctor is likely to begin treatment by behavioral intervention—changes in diet and life-style. Up to six months can be devoted to attempting nondrug therapy, and a significant number of people with hypertension can control their blood pressure without having to resort to lifetime drug intervention.

Losing weight and following a healthy diet. Being overweight increases the risk of high blood pressure anywhere from two to five times. An overweight body's excess tissue requires increased blood supply and more extensive circulation, both of which strain the heart and raise blood pressure. For overweight individuals, losing weight healthfully (without relying on drugs) is the most effective way to lower blood pressure.

Eating a diet low in fat and cholesterol will not only help control weight but may also prevent or retard arteriosclerosis. Alcohol should be drunk in moderation; it is laden with unnecessary calories, and because it is a depressant, it also reduces the efficiency of the heart's contractions. People taking prescription medications should also be careful not to mix them with alcohol.

Reducing sodium intake. Because sodium is a component of salt that contributes to water retention, consuming less salt results in less water retention. Remember that excess water and salt are stored in tissues and force the heart to work harder to circulate blood. Moderate-sodium regimens lower salt intake to one teaspoon (or 2 g of sodium) daily; people on these diets cannot add salt to their food and must avoid such processed foods as condiments, cured or smoked foods, canned foods, salty junk foods, and fast foods. Low-salt regimens in which the maximum daily intake is limited to one-quarter teaspoon of salt (or 500 mg of sodium) further reduce intake of unprocessed foods naturally high in sodium—such as dairy products.

Life-style changes. Smoking is another risk factor for CHD; quite simply, smoking cigarettes increases blood pressure and heart rate. Over time, smokers' arteries become narrow and stiff. Smokers have twice the risk of heart attack as nonsmokers and have a lower survival rate as well.

One of the healthiest practices, on the other hand, is regular exercise, which strengthens the heart, reduces the percentage of body fat, and promotes weight loss. Brisk walking, jogging, and running are all good options, reducing the rise in blood pressure that usually takes place when one is excited or stressed. Relaxation techniques such as meditation are also helpful in reducing blood pressure.

Mental exercises may also be beneficial. Meditation, for example, can induce what Dr. Herbert Benson of the Harvard Medical School calls the "relaxation response," decreasing heart rate and blood pressure. Patients can also try biofeedback. Trained instructors of this technique attach instruments that monitor and show fluctuations in blood pressure and then work to teach the patient ways to control these functions.

Drug treatment. Doctors keep several goals in mind when treating hypertension with medication. First, they must be careful not to interfere with treatment of other medical conditions. They should administer medication in as small a dosage as possible to prevent side effects and should prescribe as few drugs as possible. The number of times per day the patient needs to take medication should be as few as possible, and a step-by-step approach should be taken in finding the best combination of drugs. Doctors should also encourage patients to continue taking good care of themselves, for medication is most beneficial when a person eats healthfully, watches his or her weight, and exercises.

Drugs used to treat high blood pressure are called *antihypertensives*; these work in a variety of ways, some still not understood. Some interfere with the nervous system's transmissions to the heart, kidneys, or arteries. Among these "message interrupters" are clonidine, guanethidine, methyldopa, prazosin, rauwolfia compounds, and terazosin. Clonidine, methyldopa, and rauwolfia compounds reduce the heart's output and/or arterial resistance. Guanethidine and methyldopa cause the arteries to dilate. Common side effects of these drugs include dry mouth, drowsiness, and fatigue. Diuretics are usually prescribed with this group of drugs (for reasons discussed later).

Other classes of drugs work by preventing nervous system signals to the arteries or heart from being received. These are *betablockers*, the most frequently prescribed of which is propranolol. Beta-blockers slow down the heart rate and the force with which it beats. They tend to aggravate such respiratory conditions as asthma, emphysema, and bronchitis, however, and may also raise the cholesterol and fat levels in the bloodstream.

The third group of antihypertensives directly controls operation of the arteries, kidneys, or heart and overrides signals from the nervous system. *Hydralazine* dilates the arteries, which results in lowered blood pressure. It is usually used in conjunction with a diuretic and beta-blocker—the beta-blocker helps counter hydralazine's tendency to speed up the heartbeat. *Minoxidil* is a very strong artery dilator used for severe, advanced hypertension. It also needs to be taken with a diuretic and beta-blocker. Women on minoxidil often notice a side effect of excessive hair growth, which is reversible when they stop taking the drug.

Calcium controls contractions of smooth muscles, such as the muscle cells in arteries. *Calcium channel blockers* inhibit calcium's activity and relax muscles, especially those in the heart and arteries. These drugs do not encourage water and salt retention, so diuretics are not necessarily required.

Angiotensin-converting enzyme (ACE) inhibitors prevent the kidney from secreting renin. When renin is present in the bloodstream, it reacts with another chemical in the bloodstream called angiotensin to create angiotensin II, a powerful muscle constrictor. By controlling renin, high blood pressure levels can also be controlled. ACE inhibitors may also be used without additional diuretics.

Sympathetic nerve inhibitors prevent the nervous system from constricting arteries. Other ACE inhibitors prevent the body from manufacturing angiotensin, a substance that causes arteries to contract.

Drugs used to treat high blood pressure generally encourage the body to retain salt; thus, diuretics are frequently used. They work directly with the kidneys in one of two ways: to eliminate excess water and salt from the body or prevent their retention. Ridding the blood of excess fluid means that the heart can work less hard. A common side effect is light-headedness. Some drugs are available in combination tablets; although this decreases the number of pills one may need to take, some doctors are opposed to combinations because chances are that some component is not present in an optimal amount.

HYPERTENSION IN CHILDREN

Once a child is three years old, his or her blood pressure should be checked yearly. At birth, the infant's blood pressure is usually 65/45. From about six weeks after birth until the age of 6 years, normal blood pressure is about 90/60. After that point, it rises.

Girls show an increase in blood pressure a little earlier than boys, although the increase takes place over a greater number of years in boys.

A child with hypertension may complain of frequent headaches or have no symptoms at all. For children under the age of 12, hypertension is more likely to be secondary hypertension, possibly due to kidney disease, an enlarged kidney, or a temporary effect of a strep infection. For those over age 12, primary hypertension is more common. As with adults, too much dietary salt, obesity, and lack of exercise are contributing factors. If medication is necessary, it is given in smaller doses relative to the child's body weight.

HYPERTENSION IN WOMEN

Women who are hypertensive, overweight, have diabetes or high cholesterol, or smoke are already at higher than average risk for heart attack and stroke. Taking the Pill in addition to any or all of these life-style factors—especially for women over 35—adds to the risk.

Women who have high blood pressure before or during early pregnancy run a higher risk of delivering a low-weight or stillborn child. Because of the demands a developing baby places on the mother's circulatory system, it is normal for the pregnant woman's blood pressure to begin to elevate during the fourth month and to increase markedly during the sixth month as well. Teenage women, women over 35, and diabetic women tend to be more likely to develop hypertension in pregnancy.

Ideally, women should begin their pregnancies with blood pressures of 125/75 or less. Very mild hypertension during pregnancy can be treated by rest and by controlling salt intake. Guidelines exist to help doctors decide at what point medication should be prescribed; these include a diastolic above 90 during the first seven months, a diastolic above 95 during the seventh and eighth months, and a diastolic above 100 to 105 during the eighth and ninth months. Some medications are considered *relatively* safe for pregnant women (certain beta-blockers and alpha-methyldopa, among them). Other drugs may damage the fetus or are generally considered less safe (clonidine and diuretics) or are avoided altogether (reserpine and guanethidine, among others).

When prescribing medication for a pregnant or nursing woman, doctors weigh its benefits against possible risks to the mother and her child.

Antihypertensives that nursing mothers take vary in the degree to which they show up in breast milk. The American Association of Pediatrics has approved a few medications for nursing mothers, among them alpha-methyldopa and propranolol.

HYPERTENSION IN THE ELDERLY

As people age, their bodies become more sensitive and less able to tolerate changes in diet, exercise level, and medication. The arteries naturally become somewhat stiffer. The kidneys work less efficiently. And blood pressure will rise slightly to accommodate the effects of the aging process on the circulatory system; whereas systolic pressure rises more rapidly with age, diastolic pressure may actually decline.

An older person with high blood pressure should be treated gradually and closely monitored. Medication may need to be adjusted to a lower than usual dosage; there is an increased likelihood of side effects in the elderly, and their bodies seem more sensitive to the action of most drugs.

•   •   •   •

CHAPTER 6
. . . .
CORONARY
HEART
DISEASE

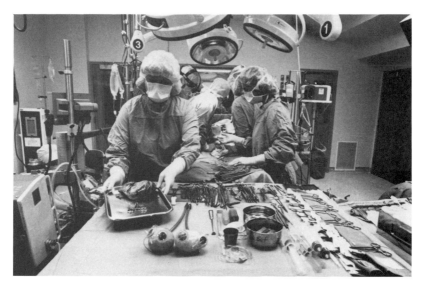

A transplant is performed for a patient whose own heart is at the point of failure.

Coronary heart diseases are often complications of arterial diseases but refer specifically to problems the heart experiences in maintaining circulation to its own muscles. Healthy heart function depends on well-conducted and -coordinated electrical impulses and on a smooth, full flow of blood through the coronary arteries. A subspecialty of cardiology called electrophysiology, the study of the electrical system of the heart, has resulted in great advances in the treatment of certain heart diseases, especially arrhythmia.

CHD results from shortages in blood supply to the heart muscle itself, which in turn is caused by blockage or narrowing of coronary arteries. This reduction in blood flow is called *ischemia*. Poor health conditions and habits, such as untreated hypertension, high levels of blood cholesterol, and cigarette smoking are major causal factors. Any one of them increases one's risk for heart disease, and in combination, the likelihood of disease skyrockets. Other medical conditions, such as diabetes, a family history of CHD, inactivity, obesity, and stress, are other contributing factors. Ischemia can also result from atherosclerosis and other arteriosclerotic conditions.

Over time, high blood pressure damages arterial walls and makes CHD a more likely outcome. The constant, intense force of blood flow damages the arteries' inner lining, wearing it away. Blood cells caught on the roughened walls stick to them and build up, clogging the artery. Ultimately, a heart attack may occur if a blood clot blocks blood flow or if pressure builds up in a clogged artery and causes it to burst.

One major symptom of CHD is *angina pectoris*, or chest pain. Often precipitated by physical exertion—during which the body has increased blood and oxygen demands that clogged arteries cannot meet—pain starts behind the breastbone, radiates through the upper chest, neck, and jaw, and may extend to the left shoulder and arm. In some cases, discomfort spreads to the right side of the body. The sensation felt is one of extreme, burning pressure. Usually a few minutes of rest will cause the pain to subside, but in severe cases discomfort lingers. Angina is a reliable indicator of heart disease; even if the pain is fleeting, it is important to seek medical treatment.

Beta-blockers, calcium channel blockers, and nitrates are all prescribed for angina. Beta-blockers help dilate blood vessels and slow down the heart rate. As their name implies, calcium channel blockers prevent calcium, responsible for muscle contractions, from being absorbed into blood vessels. Nitrates, the oldest group of drugs used to treat chest pain, work by relaxing muscle in the arteries and veins, effectively dilating them. Nitroglycerine tablets may be swallowed, held under the tongue, or worn in patch form on the chest so that the drug is absorbed through the skin.

Often, even though diseased coronary arteries reduce blood

flow to dangerously low levels, an individual will have no symptoms at all. This is known as *silent ischemia*. Usually, silent ischemia is diagnosed in the aftermath of a heart attack, during the period of EKG surveillance in the hospital.

Because each side of the heart has different functions, other symptoms of severe CHD vary with the side affected. Left heart failure causes the lungs to become congested with blood. Someone with left-heart failure develops shortness of breath and a persistent cough. Right-heart failure causes tissues in the body to become congested with blood, and edema (fluid retention) is apparent in the feet and ankles. The liver becomes somewhat enlarged, and neck veins may distend. ACE inhibitors, digitalis, and diuretics are all useful in treating congestive heart failure.

CARDIAC ARRHYTHMIAS

More than two-thirds of the 600,000 heart attack fatalities in the United States each year are attributed to cardiac arrhythmias. Some changes in heartbeat are harmless—everyone has experienced a momentary skipped beat or a racing heart. Other disturbances in which the heart beats too slowly (*bradycardia*), too quickly (*tachycardia*), or in an irregular, wildly chaotic manner (*fibrillation*), are life threatening.

Arrhythmias may occur during or after a heart attack. Other causes include heart defects and damage, CHD, and reactions to certain drugs, especially cocaine. A particularly tragic example of the latter was the 1986 death of the 22-year-old college basketball star Len Bias, who suffered a fatal, cocaine-induced arrhythmia.

In a type of arrhythmia called *ventricular tachycardia*, the ventricles contract before they have had enough time to fill with blood. Because inadequate amounts of blood are being pumped into the lungs and out of the heart, blood pressure decreases, and the individual loses consciousness and may die. *Ventricular fibrillation* is the most dangerous arrhythmia—the rhythm of ventricular contractions is so chaotic that the ventricles cannot pump blood at all. This condition is invariably fatal.

If an arrhythmia is suspected, intracardiac measurement of electrical impulses helps locate the site and source of the problem. Depending on what caused the arrhythmia, possible treatments include drugs, pacemakers, implantable defibrillators, microsurgery, and open heart surgery. Medications that treat arrhythmia include cardiac drug staples such as calcium channel blockers, beta-blockers, and digitalis. Quinidine, procainamide, and tocainide slow the electrical action of the heart. Mexiletine has an anesthetic action, and amrinone relaxes cardiac smooth muscle.

If drug treatment is ineffective, open heart surgery or catheter ablation (delivering an electric shock via catheter) can be performed to remove or selectively interrupt the area of defective conductivity. Other severe cases may be controlled by the implantation of a miniature defibrillator.

HEART ATTACK

Each year 1.5 million Americans suffer a heart attack, a prolonged, severe shortage of blood supply to the heart muscle. Another name for heart attack is *myocardial infarction*, literally, heart-muscle death. It occurs when the coronary arteries become severely narrowed and blocked by atherosclerotic plaque and blood clots.

Heart attack claimed 513,700 deaths in 1987 and is the leading cause of death for both men and women in the United States. Approximately 45% of all heart attack victims are under 65 years old. Up to age 44, men are 41 times as likely as women of the same age to have a heart attack. From 45 to 64 years old, male risk is 3 times that of female risk. After 65, women are only slightly less likely than men to experience a heart attack.

Someone having a heart attack may feel nothing, mistake the sensation for indigestion, or experience the worst pain of his or her life. A heart attack can occur at any time of day or night. It might occur out of the blue or be preceded by a feeling of general malaise. Exertion or stress may or may not precipitate its occurrence, which is signaled by pain spreading through the chest to the neck and jaw. As the heart continues to operate at less than normal capacity, the victim's body receives less and less oxygen; he or she may lose consciousness. Or the heart attack will pass, leaving its victim sweaty, pale, and shaken.

It is vital that someone having a heart attack receive medical help right away; almost half of all heart attack victims die within a few hours of their first symptoms. If the victim is unconscious and has no pulse, cardiopulmonary resuscitation (CPR) should be started immediately. CPR is a method of reviving a victim by breathing into his or her lungs to stimulate respiration and by pushing down on the sternum to manually force circulation. Most heart attack fatalities occur because the heart has become ar-rhythmic, which prevents blood from being circulated within the heart and around the body. Electrical defibrillation is used to restart and stabilize the heart: A small paddle is placed on either side of the heart, and an electrical current is passed from one to the other through the heart. This usually shocks the heart out of its aberrant rhythm and back into regular beats. Ambulances now have defibrillators, so if need be, this can be done before arrival at the hospital.

Once in the hospital, most heart attack patients are placed in a specialized coronary care unit. Intravenous fluids are started, blood samples are drawn, and the patient is hooked up to an EKG machine for continuous monitoring of the heart's electrical activity and heartbeat. Respiration rate and blood pressure may also be continually monitored, and supplementary oxygen is available if needed. No lingering symptoms may be present, or the patient may feel weak and experience trouble breathing. An-other patient may suffer a recurrent arrhythmia.

Depending on a patient's condition, drugs are given to prevent arrhythmias, break up and prevent blood clots, maintain heart rate, dilate blood vessels, and reduce fluid buildup. A wide range of diagnostic techniques is used to determine the exact location and extent of damage to the heart muscle. Among them are stan-dard, Holter, and stress EKGs and imaging techniques, including X rays, MRI, and echocardiography.

Clot dissolvers, such as streptokinase, urokinase, or the still-experimental *recombinant tissue plasminogen activator* (rt-PA), if administered within a few hours of the heart attack, are very effective in unblocking arteries and can save lives. Often the next step in treatment is coronary arteriography to locate the site of the blockage, followed by angioplasty, or surgical arterial clean-ing, to dilate the clogged artery.

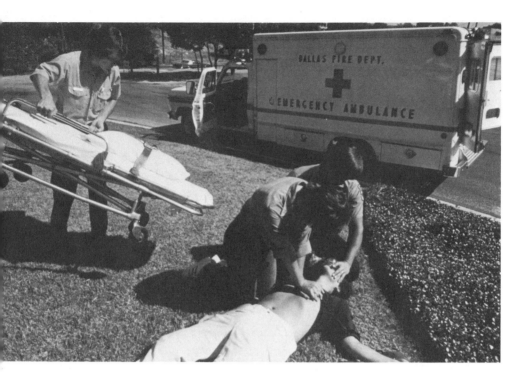

In an emergency, cardiopulmonary resuscitation (CPR) can be used to revive victims of a heart attack before they get to a hospital.

The recent multicenter "Thrombolysis in Myocardial Infarction" (TIMI) Trial, sponsored by the National Heart, Lung, and Blood Institute, has provided valuable information about the effectiveness of different strategies in treating heart attack. Initial findings published in the July 1987 issue of *Circulation* revealed that rt-PA was twice as successful as streptokinase in unclogging arteries. In November 1987 the *Journal of the American College of Cardiology* reported that angioplasty to dilate a clogged artery works well and may be safely performed after rt-PA therapy. The *American Journal of Cardiology* reported in its March 1, 1989, issue that rt-PA also helps maintain good left-ventricle function after a heart attack. A final report of the TIMI study in the March 9, 1989, *New England Journal of Medicine* endorses a conservative strategy of using clot dissolvers first and delaying coronary arteriography and angioplasty rather than automatically following up clot dissolvers with these invasive tactics.

Coronary artery bypass is another treatment option. If the heart has been severely damaged and can no longer beat efficiently, a pacemaker may be implanted. Sometimes heart attack with loss of breathing results in brain damage and possibly death; the likelihood of survival depends on the age of the person involved and the cause of cardiac arrest.

DIAGNOSING AND TREATING
CORONARY HEART DISEASE

At one time, heart conditions were almost invariably fatal. But advances in medical knowledge as well as sophisticated technological developments have made diagnosing and treating heart conditions possible.

Cardiopulmonary Resuscitation (CPR)

When a person falls unconscious, as he or she might as a result of cardiac shock, heart attack, or arrhythmia, the first response should be to determine whether or not he or she is breathing or has a pulse. If the victim is unresponsive, is not breathing, and has no pulse, CPR should be performed immediately to force air into the lungs and reestablish the heartbeat. Defibrillation may be necessary to reestablish a heartbeat or treat an arrhythmia.

Exercise Electrocardiography

Doctors will use exercise electrocardiography, also known as an exercise or stress test, to check adequacy of blood flow in the coronary arteries. A stress test is often performed to help diagnose coronary heart disease before a sedentary individual begins an exercise program or to measure progress after a heart attack or following a particular treatment procedure. A physical exam, blood pressure reading, and resting EKG are performed right before starting this test. The patient exercises on a stationary bike, treadmill, or steps while hooked up to an EKG machine for simultaneous observation via a heart monitor. Blood pressure and pulse are frequently checked. The speed of the exercise machine regularly increases, and the heart's response to this is closely monitored. An *electroencephalogram*, or EEG, in which electrodes placed on the patient's scalp pick up impulses transmitted and received by brain cells, measures the brain's electrical activity and can be done at the same time and analyzed later. Sometimes a radioactive substance like thallium is injected into the patient's body before the test so that any blockages in the coronary arteries can be located.

Angioplasty

One way of treating atherosclerosis in coronary arteries and arteries leading to the kidneys and legs is *angioplasty*, in which the clogged or blocked artery is manually dilated or cleaned out.

In 1977 a Swiss doctor, Andreas Gruentzig, successfully used a balloon-catheter method to enlarge coronary arteries. This method represents a major therapeutic advance and is now becoming a common procedure. In 1987, 184,000 angioplasties were performed in the United States.

With the patient under local anesthesia, a catheter is guided through a major artery until it reaches the opening to the coronary artery. Another smaller catheter is inserted through the first one. The innermost catheter contains a tiny balloon that is inflated to crush the plaque blocking the artery into a thin layer, dilating the artery. The balloon may be inflated and kept in place for anywhere from several seconds to several minutes. When the artery is satisfactorily opened, the balloon is deflated and the catheters are withdrawn.

In up to 5% of all angioplasties, an artery closes off completely during or right after the procedure. If this happens, an emergency bypass may be performed. In about 25% of all angioplasties, the artery is subject to *restinosis*, or renarrowing. If the artery remains open and dilated for the first year following the procedure, chances are the artery will present no problems in the future. Another angioplasty method currently being tested uses a laser beam to burn away fatty deposits in a blocked artery. Streptokinase may also be injected via catheter into clogged arteries to distend them.

Angioplasty is not the only option for people with atherosclerosis; bypass surgery and/or drug therapy are better alternatives in situations in which minor arteries or smaller branches are blocked. In *endarterectomy*, an artery is surgically opened and the blockage manually removed.

PACEMAKERS AND OTHER IMPLANTABLE DEVICES

Electronic pacemakers have meant the difference between life and death for approximately 400,000 people worldwide (200,000 of them in the United States) whose hearts beat irregularly or too infrequently to adequately circulate blood through their bodies.

All pacemakers have a unit for generating impulses, plus one or more wires that transport these signals to the heart. Three kinds of pacemakers are on the market now. The most common is the *single-chamber* unit. With the patient under local anesthetic, a small pocket for the pacemaker is surgically created in the chest wall, in the upper portion of the right breast area. Its insulated wire electrode is threaded through a vein and inserted into the tip of the right ventricle. This method of implantation is known as the *transvenous method*.

The pacemaker can sense a normal heartbeat and will not send an electrical charge through the heart as long as a normal heartbeat is present. This is an *on-demand* pacemaker. When the heart pauses for too long, the pacemaker sends an impulse to the right ventricle and the heart contracts. On-demand pacemakers are sensitive to metal-detector emissions, mistaking them for the heart's electrical impulses and temporarily shutting down. Electrical tools should be used with caution by people with this type of pacemaker.

Dual-chamber pacemakers are more sophisticated than single-chamber ones. They work by mimicking the beating heart: First they contract the upper chambers, allow a brief pause for blood to be pumped to the ventricles, and then produce another contraction to open the aortic and pulmonary valves. The dual-chamber pacemaker has two wires. One is run into the right atrium; the other, into the right ventricle.

The automatic implantable cardioverter defibrillator (AICD) shocks the heart to restore normal heart rhythms. Using a method of implantation called an epicardial implant, the electrode is placed directly on the heart's surface, and the generator is inserted in an under-the-skin pocket.

CORONARY ARTERY BYPASS SURGERY

If angioplasty is not effective or appropriate for a life-threatening coronary blockage, coronary artery bypass is another remedy. In 1987, approximately 332,000 people in the United States underwent bypass surgery. The technique for coronary bypass was developed in the 1960s by Drs. Michael Debakey and Edward Garrett, who used a section of a patient's leg vein to bypass a damaged section of artery.

In bypass surgery, the patient is anesthetized and hooked up to a heart-lung machine, and the heart is infused with a cold solution to keep it from beating. Veins taken from elsewhere in the body are sewn into the heart to bypass the area of arterial blockage. One end of each vein is sewn in front of the blockage, and the other is sewn directly into the aorta. More than one bypass can be performed at a time.

Within about three months, bypass patients return to their regular routines, with the majority experiencing some, if not total, relief from angina.

HEART TRANSPLANT

A suitable candidate for heart transplant is a person with severe, otherwise untreatable congestive heart failure or one with a primary disease of the heart muscle who is in otherwise good health. Patients with cancer, an active infection, or diabetes cannot be considered for transplant because the immunosuppressive drugs necessary following surgery aggravate these conditions.

Donor hearts usually come from people under 45 years old who have died from hemorrhage or injury to the brain and are free from communicable diseases. Blood type, immune-response antigens, and antibodies between donor and recipient must be as similar as possible. Once the donor heart is removed from the body, it can be stored for up to two days before reimplantation.

The recipient is put on antibiotics and immunosuppressives to prepare his or her body for the transplant. Surgeons will

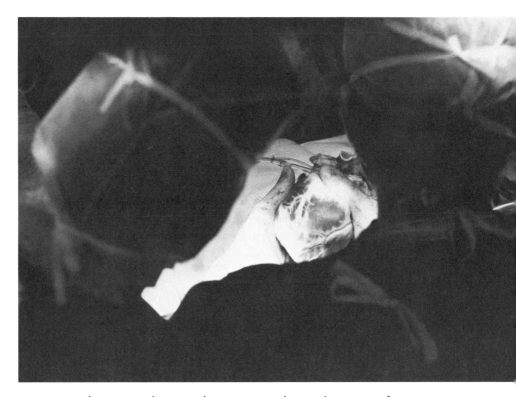

Heart transplants can take many hours to complete, using organs from donors who have died from injuries that did not affect the heart.

anesthetize the patient, then open the chest and connect the body to a heart-lung machine. The pericardium is opened and the heart removed, leaving the back of the atrial wall intact so that the new heart may be reconnected to it. The recipient's pulmonary artery and aorta are severed close to the heart and are rejoined to these vessels in the donor's heart. The entire procedure takes from 5 to 10 hours, although the actual transplant takes only an hour or so.

Recovery usually proceeds quickly, with the patient walking within two days and on an exercise bicycle within another day. Care is taken to prevent infection, for the immunosuppressive drugs so vital to the new heart's acceptance in the patient's body also leave it defenseless. Doctors will also look carefully for evidence of organ rejection, hemorrhage, clot formation, and impairment of cardiovascular function. The patient will have to take immunosuppressives for the rest of his or her life. If all goes well, the patient is discharged from the hospital in about two weeks and within three months may return to normal activities. Treatment does not end with a successful transplant; regular follow-up examinations and medication become a permanent part of the patient's new life.

MECHANICAL CIRCULATORY SUPPORT

Intraaortic balloon counterpulsation (IABC) is used to boost a weak heartbeat after a heart attack, during invasive procedures if the patient has a history of ischemia, and during heart failure. This device was perfected by Dr. Adrian Kantrowitz at Maimonides Medical Center in Brooklyn, New York, in 1967. Inserted into the aorta with the help of a catheter, the balloon is attached to an external air pump. Rhythmic inflation pushes blood through the aorta. Patients can stay on IABC for up to two weeks.

Some patients require more than IABC; *left ventricular assist devices* (LVAD) are used to provide temporary pumping support after surgery, whereas the artificial heart is for longer periods while the heart is still recuperating or for patients experiencing heart failure who are waiting for donor hearts. In temporary LVAD, a tube inserted into the left ventricle allows blood to flow into an artificial, external "left ventricle." A power supply attached to the artificial chamber pumps the blood from it back into the aorta via a second tube. Permanent LVAD, in which the artificial ventricle and/or the power supply are completely implanted in the patient's body, are under development by researchers at a variety of universities and biotechnology companies, including Dr. Willem J. Kolff and his team at the University of Utah's Division of Artificial Organs and Dr. Peer M. Portner of Andors, Inc., in Berkeley, California.

•   •   •   •

CHAPTER 7

· · · · · · · · · · · · · · ·

STROKE

Stroke afflicts a half million Americans each year.

Stroke is the third leading cause of death in the United States. According to the American Heart Association, about a half million men and women in this country suffer stroke each year; in more than 25% of these cases, the stroke is fatal. Survivors are usually disabled, and many can no longer live independently but require care at home or in a nursing home. About 2 million Americans are currently disabled by stroke.

Another term for stroke is *cerebrovascular accident*—a term that reflects perceptions that stroke is something uncontrollable that happens out of the blue. Many older people are still fearful of impending stroke and the disability and dependence stroke causes. It is now known that stroke is a common outcome of many years of untreated hypertension and unhealthy habits—fatty diet, lack of exercise, cigarette smoking, and excessive alcohol consumption. It is much easier to prevent stroke than rehabilitate a stroke survivor. Stroke fatalities in the United States alone have decreased by 50% since 1968, an improvement mostly attributable to control of hypertension.

Stroke is a cardiovascular disease that affects blood vessels of the central nervous system. When adequate amounts of oxygen cannot reach the brain, brain cells die, and the part of the body those cells control ceases to function normally. To understand how stroke occurs and its effects on the brain, one should take a closer look at how the healthy brain functions.

THE BRAIN

The brain is the topmost end of the central nervous system and contains the most important nerves for the head. It is also the seat of all conscious mental functioning: the ability to think, use language, process sensory information, feel, move, be. As such, the brain is richly supplied with blood vessels that provide it with a steady supply of vital oxygen from the blood.

Parts of the Brain

The largest and uppermost part of the brain, the cerebrum, is the center of intellectual activity. It runs from eye level at the front of the head to the back of the head and is divided into two separate sections called the *right* and *left cerebral hemispheres*. Seen from above, the cerebrum looks like a shelled walnut half.

Almost 20% of the blood leaving the heart goes to the brain. The *left* and *right carotid arteries* are the main vessels that supply the brain's cerebral hemispheres—the seat of all conscious mental processes. Whereas the left carotid artery branches out directly from the aorta, the right carotid artery is an outgrowth of another main branch, the innominate. "Carotid" comes from the Greek word *karas*, meaning drowsy, which is exactly how one feels if pressure is applied to these arteries. The brain stem, cerebellum, and the rear of the cerebral hemispheres are served by the vertebral arteries. The *circle of Willis*, formed by these and other arteries at the brain's base, is named after Thomas Willis, the English physician who first described them in 1664.

The ancient Greeks realized correctly that each hemisphere controls the opposite side of the body; the left brain controls the right side of the body, and vice versa. Sensory nerve fibers and motor fibers pass through both halves of the brain.

Each hemisphere specializes in different functions. The left hemisphere almost always contains speech and language centers. A right-handed person is said to be *left-brain dominant*. Most left-handed people are left-brain dominant, too. Occasionally, a left-handed person's speech and language center will be in his or her right brain. The right brain normally contains spatial, perceptual, and motor centers responsible for a variety of skills, among them the ability to recognize faces, feel and express emotion, and recall the melody of a particular song.

Natural fissures, or grooves, in the brain's surface led scientists to divide the brain into four *lobes*, or sections. The *frontal lobe* begins at above eye level and continues back to the top of the head; the *parietal lobe* begins at the top of the head and ranges down a few inches; the *occipital lobe* is the section toward the back of the head; and the *temporal lobe* lies on either side of the head above the ears. The general location of the areas that control speech, motor, sensory, and visual capacities have also been pinpointed.

The right frontal lobe is responsible for emotion and personality. Eye movement and the sense of smell are also controlled by this lobe. The left frontal lobe contains *Broca's speech area*—involved in the ability to initiate speech, choose words, and form sentences.

Directly behind the frontal lobe lies a groove called the *fissure of Rolando*. The motor area, meaning the area that controls body movements, lies in front of this groove. The body parts it affects are arranged in an upside-down order: Whereas the section closest to the top of the head affects the leg area, the head and face are controlled by a section at the area's bottom near the side of the head. The sensory area lies behind the fissure of Rolando and is responsible for sensations of touch and pain. Because it receives sensations of pressure on the joints in the body, the sensory area helps guide the movements of the limbs. The sensory area also has an upside-down arrangement.

Mathematical calculation and *constructional* ability—the ability to envision an object—are controlled by the left parietal lobe. The right parietal area is involved with awareness and use of the left side of the body. The occipital lobe includes the area of the brain responsible for processing what we see. Each eye has both an inner and outer visual field. The right visual area receives information from the left sides of both eyes, and vice versa.

The temporal lobe contains *Wernicke's speech area*, which is involved in receiving speech—comprehending what people are saying and remembering it—and understanding the written word.

STROKE

Disruption of blood flow to the brain, which precipitates stroke, may be caused by a blood clot, a narrowed or clogged artery, or a hemorrhage. Starved of oxygen, nerve cells in the brain quickly die, and functions controlled by those cells are lost, often permanently. The majority of strokes take place in the cerebral hemisphere and usually occur only in one side of the brain.

About 80% of all strokes are caused by one of two types of clots: *cerebral thrombosis* occurs when a blood clot forms in an artery that supplies part of the brain; this is the most common type of stroke. Cerebral thrombotic strokes usually occur early in the morning or during the night. In *cerebral embolism*, the blood clot is formed elsewhere in the body, then carried in the bloodstream to a brain artery, where it blocks blood flow.

Sometimes stroke will follow a heart attack. While the heart undergoes its healing process, a blood clot can form and lodge in an artery feeding the brain. Anticoagulant therapy given after a heart attack reduces the chances of this occurring. Any heart disease that slows the circulation of blood will increase the chances of clot formation and hence the incidence of stroke.

When blood vessels rupture, they hemorrhage—or bleed—into the surrounding area. Although hemorrhage is a less frequent cause of stroke, the extreme pressure hemorrhage exerts on the brain results in a higher fatality rate.

Cerebral hemorrhage is bleeding within the brain tissue as a result of a head injury or a burst *aneurysm*, a weak spot on a blood vessel's surface. More than 300 years ago, the Swiss doctor Johann Jacob Wepfer published an account of four cases of stroke in which he mentions cerebral hemorrhage as the cause. If a blood vessel on the surface of the brain ruptures, it is known as a *subarachnoid hemorrhage*. Subarachnoid hemorrhages bleed into the area between the brain and the skull. Although the fatality rate is high, those who survive hemorrhage-induced strokes regain more of their faculties than those who live through other strokes.

High blood pressure is a factor in both clot- and hemorrhage-induced strokes. Over time, high blood pressure damages arterial walls. Usually smooth and supple, the arteries' inner lining is damaged and destroyed by the constant, accelerated force of blood flow. Not only does the lining become roughened; it wears away, exposing the underlying tissue. Blood cells get caught on the roughened walls and stick to them. As blood cells build up, they clog the artery; if this happens in an artery that supplies the brain, a stroke is likely to follow. If pressure builds up in a clogged artery, it may burst and hemorrhage.

Strokes usually take place quite gradually, over a period of a day or two rather than over hours. Timely treatment may prevent the stroke from developing further. In 10% of strokes, forewarning occurs in the form of a *transient ischemic attack* (TIA), or "ministroke." TIAs are the result of a temporary blood clot in an artery leading to the brain. A ministroke's effects last less than 24 hours—more than 75% of them last less than 5 minutes, leaving no permanent damage. Even though a TIA is over quickly and does not impair its victim, it is important that someone experiencing unusual symptoms see a doctor right away.

Another type of stroke is classified as a *reversible ischemic neurological deficit*. It is distinct from a TIA in that its effects last longer than 24 hours, but those who suffer from it will fully recover within several weeks.

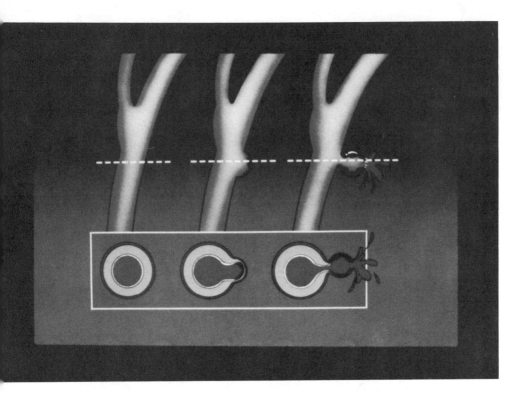

Aneurysms form when the tissue of the heart or its blood vessels have been weakened and start to swell. In extreme cases the blood vessels may even burst.

Warning Signs and Symptoms

Even though the warning signs of stroke and TIA are similar to symptoms of other disorders, it is vitally important that anyone experiencing them receive immediate medical help. Symptoms of stroke often vary depending on the cause and location of the stroke. General symptoms of strokes due to insufficient blood to the brain include: faint vision, especially in one eye; inability or difficulty in speaking and comprehending speech; sudden numbness or weakness of the arm, leg, or face on one side of the body; and sudden dizziness with no apparent cause.

Cerebral hemorrhage has a rapid onset; the victim might complain of a severe headache, start vomiting, and soon afterward lose consciousness. This type of stroke is usually fatal. Someone experiencing a subarachnoid hemorrhage will also suffer a severe headache and vomiting. Half these cases are fatal; they are generally caused by an aneurysm, a weakened area of the blood vessel that bursts.

Although stroke most commonly affects the cerebral hemispheres, some occur at the base of the brain, or the *brain stem*. Weakness in the limbs and problems with coordination are not limited to one side of the body in such strokes, and lack of eye-movement control is also common. Hemorrhage is a rare cause of stroke in this area but is usually fatal. If the patient survives a brain-stem stroke, recovery is usually good.

Another type of stroke, *vertebrobasilar insufficiency*, has a particularly dramatic onset: Its victims fall to the floor unconscious but usually recover completely in a few minutes. In this form of stroke the neck's section of the spine becomes arthritic and exerts pressure on arteries that supply blood to the brain. If an individual with arthritis in this area turns his or her head suddenly or leans back for a shampoo by a hairdresser, an attack of unconsciousness might immediately follow.

Another possible source of stroke is injury to the head, which may result in a blood clot between the brain and its outer membrane. It may be months before the blood clot causes problems, but the symptoms are very similar to those of stroke—headache, weakness on one side of the body, and drowsiness. When the onset of what appears to be a stroke is gradual, a brain tumor is also suspected.

Strokes in children are rare and tend to have very different causes than do those in adults. Infections like malaria and meningitis can spread to the arteries that lead to the brain, causing inflammation. Or a child might accidentally swallow a pen or pencil, which may then pierce the carotid artery in the neck. An active phase of sickle cell anemia, during which blood is likely to clot, might also precipitate a stroke.

Many people are conscious during their strokes, and if they maintain a normal level of consciousness for the first 48 hours, they have an 85% chance of survival and recovery. Those who become very drowsy, lose voluntary eye movement, and fall into a coma—all signs of swelling of and pressure on the brain—are more likely to die.

The symptoms experienced while various types of strokes are

in progress—numbness in a limb, inability to use language in one way or another, paralysis of one side of the body—are often the limitations the victim is left to overcome once the stroke has run its course and has reached its maximum stage of damage.

Diagnosis

Sometimes stroke victims seek out medical care immediately; others may wait a day or so. If stroke is suspected, the victim should go to the hospital as soon as possible. What caused the stroke, what part of the brain it affected, ways to prevent further damage, and what the patient is capable of following the stroke need to be determined. One of the most pressing questions on everyone's mind is to what extent the patient will recover and return to his or her normal life and activities. Age, general health, location, and extent of brain damage all affect the prognosis.

The doctor quickly takes information about what has just occurred and the individual's general medical history, measures blood pressure and pulse, checks the patient's heart and eyes, and uses a stethoscope to listen for abnormal sounds produced by a clogged carotid artery.

Once stroke is suspected, a doctor needs to determine the patient's levels of memory, orientation, capacity to use language, and consciousness. An eye test is given to check if vision has been affected. Hearing in both ears is tested, as is the patient's ability to locate the source of sound. Perception of pain is checked by pricking the limbs, face, and body with a clean pin. Degree of sensitivity to touch can be checked by having the patient immerse his or her hand in warm and cold water. Reflexes, mobility of fingers and toes, and muscular strength are also tested. Simple tests, questions, and conversation can tell the doctor a good deal about the stroke survivor's condition.

Lab tests, including a blood test, an EKG, and a chest X ray, are commonly done. The presence of certain enzymes in the blood is a giveaway that stroke has occurred. An EKG is useful in pinpointing heart problems or a recent heart attack that might have led to the stroke; a chest X ray also indicates the heart's condition. To help determine the stroke's cause, a sample of fluid normally present in the cerebrospinal canal is taken. Cerebrospinal fluid is usually clear; if the sample is bloody, chances are good that the stroke was caused by a hemorrhage.

To help pinpoint the area affected by stroke and determine the extent of the damage, a variety of sophisticated tests can be run. Assessing blood flow to and through the brain provides useful information. Ultrasound can detect arterial narrowing and blockages. A sensitive microphone can pick up abnormal sound, and blood pressure in the eyes can be measured to assess blood flow to the brain. A standard angiogram provides an image of the brain's major blood vessels and clarifies the presence and location of blockages.

The brain's electrical activity can be tested with an electroencephalogram. An *evoked response* test measures how well the brain responds to sensory stimulation. Useful images of the brain are made using *computer axial tomography* (also known as a *CAT scan*). In this technique, X-ray pictures of the brain are taken from many different angles. These individual pictures are fed into a computer, which then generates a three-dimensional composite. In magnetic resonance imaging, a magnetic field is used to create an image of the brain.

If the stroke seems still to be evolving and caused by a blood clot, anticoagulants may be given to dissolve the clot. Because they can aggravate internal bleeding, anticoagulants are not given unless it is known for certain that hemorrhage did not cause the stroke.

A carotid endarterectomy, surgery in which the carotid artery is opened so that plaque can be removed, is sometimes performed. But its effectiveness in preventing another stroke depends on the amount of arteriosclerosis present in arteries elsewhere in the body. Because aspirin is a blood thinner, it is sometimes prescribed for those at high risk of heart attack and stroke. A study conducted at the Bowman Grey School of Medicine in Winston-Salem, North Carolina, determined that carotid endarterectomy plus aspirin therapy will prevent TIA and stroke in subjects with evidence of carotid artery stenosis.

The Effects of Stroke

Individuals who have experienced a stroke are all affected differently by it, depending on the type of stroke and where in the brain it occurred. *Hemianesthesia* is the loss of sensation in limbs on the same side of the body. Stroke may also result in *hemiparesis*, weakness of one side of the body. In more severe cases, limbs on one side of the body are completely paralyzed; this is called *hemiplegia*.

Problems using speech are also common. *Aphasia* is impaired ability to use words and symbols for ideas. An individual may have *expressive* aphasia, or difficulty in speaking. *Receptive* aphasia refers to difficulty in understanding spoken language. A stroke victim who has difficulty speaking clearly is said to have *dysarthria*. Also possible is the loss of sight in either the left or right sides of both eyes—*homonymous hemianopia*.

After a stroke, one's sensory information may become garbled, memories become dim, and customary patterns of behavior change. Feeling out of control of one's body and mind is frightening and frustrating for both the patient and those around him or her. As one stroke survivor, Agnes de Mille, was quoted in *How to Prevent a Stroke*,

> there were . . . irrational and insane jerkings which I was not aware of. My hand would fly out and encounter, well, whatever there was to encounter. . . . Training that right hand to do the most primitive bidding was like training a wild animal. . . It was not my hand. It was not anybody's hand. It could have been the hind leg of a donkey. (10–11)

Determining the extent of a stroke's damage can be painstaking. The sense organs may be perfectly functional, but the ability to accurately interpret sensory information may still be impaired. A stroke survivor who can clearly hear a question may not be able to understand it unless it is presented in written form. Or perhaps he or she understands spoken language but is unable to reply verbally. It can take patience and creativity on the part of medical staff, the patient, and family and friends to figure out and master the form of communication the individual understands and the forms of communication he or she is able to use, whether verbal, written, or gestural. The first week after the stroke is the time of most rapid recovery, although lost skills may be regained slowly over time.

Depression is common after stroke and is a normal emotional reaction to the change in one's life. Stroke survivors often grieve for who they used to be before accepting themselves as they have become. Counseling can be effective in helping lift the survivor out of depression. Antidepressant drugs are helpful but require careful monitoring for side effects. Sometimes damage to the brain causes emotional lability, in which the survivor cries or laughs inappropriately and uncontrollably. Over time, lability subsides. Brain injury may also cause extreme personality changes; someone who was quiet before a stroke might be gregarious afterward.

Treatment and Rehabilitation

For those who survive stroke, the central question is how well they can overcome their impairment. The issues of independence and the patient's ability to lead a productive life are on many people's mind: the patient, family and friends, the doctor, and the rehabilitation team.

A good rehabilitation program is invaluable for teaching stroke victims and their families strategies for making day-to-day life easier. Relearning how best to use both the impaired and unimpaired parts of the body and how to eat, dress, go to the bathroom, and keep clean are some of the basics of therapy.

Risk Factors and Prevention

Once physical and/or mental damage from a stroke occurs, there is no complete cure. It is important to adopt a healthier life-style and do what is possible to prevent stroke from recurring.

Risk of stroke increases with age, and men are more likely than women to suffer one. Diabetes increases the risk of stroke, especially for women. Black Americans run a 60% higher risk of death and disability from stroke than do whites. Those who have had one stroke are at much higher risk of experiencing another, and people who have a family history of stroke are also at higher risk, as are those who have *asymptomatic carotid bruit*, or atherosclerosis of the carotid artery resulting in an abnormal sound called *bruit* that can be heard through a stethoscope.

Risk Factors Within Our Control

The primary risk factor for stroke is high blood pressure, and the higher one's blood pressure is, the higher the risk of stroke. Fortunately, hypertension is controllable, sometimes by diet and weight loss alone, sometimes with drugs as well.

Heart disease also increases the likelihood of stroke. Reducing the risk of heart disease involves lowering blood cholesterol levels and controlling blood pressure. A high red blood count is another risk factor for stroke; the higher the number of red blood cells in the bloodstream, the more likely blood is to thicken and clot.

The best long-term insurance against stroke is to lead as healthy and active a life-style as possible. Maintaining a low-fat diet, not smoking, keeping alcohol intake low, exercising, and controlling weight are the best ways to become and remain healthy.

•   •   •   •

CHAPTER 8
· · · · · · · · · · · · · · · · ·
PREVENTION
AND THE
FUTURE

A healthy diet does not have to be flavorless.

During the past 50 years scientists have made great strides in understanding and treating cardiovascular disease. Even though coronary artery disease, hypertension, and stroke often prove fatal, they can be prevented by good health habits, just as the cardiovascular disorders caused by infections can often be cured simply by early detection. Corrective surgery has succeeded in revising the heart's physical structures to the point where almost any defect can be corrected.

The future holds promise for more effective treatments, many of which use biologically derived substances, and for preventive techniques that go to the source of many disorders—the genetic code. Ultimately, medical science seeks not only a better cure but to understand and eliminate disease altogether.

PREVENTION

In 1948, 5,000 residents of Framingham, Massachusetts, a small town near Boston, began their participation in a U.S. government study to investigate the causes of heart disease. For 30 years, their medical histories, living habits, and causes of death were compiled and analyzed. The Framingham study found that heart disease is largely a man-made phenomenon: cigarette smoking, high blood pressure, and high levels of blood cholesterol all lead to increased risk of heart disease.

These findings are reflected in the American Heart Association's guidelines for reducing the risk of cardiovascular disease, which in general prescribes eating a diet low in fats and salt, not smoking, controlling hypertension, getting regular exercise, and maintaining a healthy weight.

Low-fat Regimen

Cholesterol is a substance in food that has got a lot of attention recently. Labels on packaged foods assert that they are "naturally low in cholesterol" or "contain no cholesterol." Many people are on diets to reduce their cholesterol levels.

Why all the fuss? Since almost the beginning of the 20th century, studies have shown that high levels of cholesterol in the diet are linked to an increased risk of cardiovascular disease. But in 1984, the results of a 10-year study, the Lipid Research Clinics Coronary Primary Prevention Trials (LRC CPPT), conducted by the National Institutes of Health showed that lowering cholesterol levels with drugs and a low-fat diet reduces the chance of suffering a heart attack or heart disease. (It should be noted that the LRC CPPT, like most studies of factors associated with heart disease, used only middle-aged men as experimental subjects. Study results were then generalized to apply to men and women, children, and the elderly. It is still unknown to what extent cholesterol is related to cardiovascular disease in children, women, and the elderly.)

Cholesterol is a type of *lipid*, or fat, found in the body. There is nothing inherently bad about fats; in fact, fats are vital to the body's healthy functioning. Lipids combine with proteins so that they can travel in the bloodstream and be utilized by the body; in this state they are called *lipoproteins*.

There are three types of cholesterol: *Low-density lipoprotein*, or *LDL*, is "bad" cholesterol. It is stored in the body's tissues and is the form of cholesterol that clogs arteries. *High-density lipoprotein*, or *HDL*, is "good" cholesterol. It actually fights the formation of fat in the arteries and transports cholesterol through the blood and back to the liver, where it can be broken down and excreted through the intestines. *Very low density lipoprotein*, or *VLDL*, is the precursor to LDL. Triglycerides are another blood lipid correlated with arteriosclerosis.

Where does cholesterol come from and why is it needed? Production of hormones and body tissues depends on the presence of cholesterol. Cholesterol is actually produced in human bodies and in the bodies of all animals, including fish and birds; this native cholesterol is known as *endogenous* cholesterol. The human body produces enough cholesterol to take care of its own needs. When foods of animal origin are eaten, the cholesterol in the food source is ingested. This is called *exogenous* cholesterol and is mostly excess cholesterol that clogs the arterial walls, leading to atherosclerosis and heart disease. Thus, reducing cholesterol intake can significantly improve health. Cholesterol levels can be measured by taking a blood sample. LDL cannot be measured directly, but its level can be inferred from total cholesterol, HDL, and triglyceride measurements. Eggs, whole-milk dairy products, butter, chicken skin, and animal fats are all high in cholesterol and should be eaten sparingly. Better choices are skim-milk dairy products, some margarines, skinless chicken, and fish.

Saturated fats also raise blood cholesterol levels. One can usually tell if a fat is saturated if it is solid at room temperature, like Crisco. Any food from animal sources is high in saturated fats. Coconut and palm oils are exceptions to the rule; though they are liquid at room temperature, they are still saturated fats.

Polyunsaturated fats actually lower blood cholesterol levels. Fish oils and most vegetable oils are polyunsaturates; one clue is that they are liquid at room temperature. To make them solid at room temperature, polyunsaturates are *hydrogenated*, chemically combined with hydrogen. They can be completely or partially hydrogenated. Margarine is an example of a partially hydrogenated fat but is still considered a polysaturate. If a polysaturate is completely hydrogenated, though, it behaves like a saturated fat and raises blood cholesterol.

Monounsaturates are another type of unsaturate; they neither raise nor lower blood cholesterol. Olive oil and peanut butter are monounsaturates.

Many foods contain more than one type of fat. A good rule of thumb for determining acceptable foods is to check labels. If the food has at least twice as much polyunsaturated fat as saturated fat, eating it will not increase one's blood cholesterol level. Current recommendations suggest that cholesterol levels should be monitored from the age of 2 years onward and that no more than 250 to 300 mg of cholesterol should be consumed daily. Total fat consumption should not exceed 30% of one's daily caloric intake and should be derived equally from saturated, polyunsaturated, and monounsaturated sources. Individuals with high blood pressure are put on moderate- to low-salt diets. But even if one's blood pressure is normal, it makes sense to break the salty junk-food habit.

Smoking

According to the Framingham study, cigarette smoking is the primary risk factor for CHD: Smokers have twice the risk of heart attack as nonsmokers, and they are also less likely to survive a heart attack. Smoking has damaging short-term effects, too: While someone puffs on a cigarette, nicotine speeds up the heartbeat, and carbon dioxide starves the heart of oxygen. The person's blood becomes thicker, stickier, and more likely to form clots. Blood pressure rises and blood vessels constrict. If an individual is already a cigarette smoker, he or she should quit. Not smoking may be the single best way to prevent cardiovascular diseases and lung cancer.

Body Weight

Being overweight strains the heart and raises blood pressure. Overweight people are also more likely to have high cholesterol and diabetes. For overweight individuals, losing weight is the most reliable, nondrug way to lower blood pressure.

Stress

Stress is the human reaction to changes in the environment, whether good or bad. Each person has a different tolerance level to life's events; what one finds exhilarating, another might find anxiety provoking.

Stress is not a modern invention. When prehistoric beings confronted a predator, the tension and dry mouth that impelled them to turn and run involved the same rush of adrenaline and other hormones that flood the body when one is faced with a traffic jam, an argument, a difficult exam, a blind date, or making a sales presentation. But this fight-or-flight reaction, as it has been called, does not work as well for modern-day people in contemporary situations.

Ultimately, this triggering of higher pulse, blood pressure, and heart-rate levels may have destructive effects on the cardiovascular system, especially in someone under stress for long periods. Instead of returning to normalcy, his or her body enters a permanent state of stress, with a pounding heart, high blood pressure, and constricted blood vessels.

Exercise

Exercise strengthens the heart, lowers the percentage of body fat, promotes weight loss, and reduces stress. In 1987, after analyzing the results of 43 other studies, Carl J. Casperson and Kenneth Powell of the Centers for Disease Control found that physically inactive people face as much of a heart attack risk as those who have hypertension or high cholesterol or smoke cigarettes.

Regular Medical Checkups

The American Heart Association stresses that adults should be regularly screened for high blood pressure, high cholesterol, and diabetes. Thorough checkups should begin when a person is 20 years old and should be repeated at least every 5 years, or more often if there are medical conditions that require more frequent monitoring. A family history of diabetes, high cholesterol, hypertension, or heart disease makes checkups even more important. Blood pressure should be checked every two years. Women who take contraceptive pills should have yearly checkups because pill use increases their risk of heart disease and stroke, especially if they smoke cigarettes.

WHAT IS IN STORE FOR THE FUTURE?

Excellent medical technology exists to assess brain damage after a stroke, but very few ways to prevent or treat stroke currently exist. Experiments are currently under way at the University of

Regular checkups include blood pressure readings and, as the patient ages, EKGs and blood tests. All these are important tools in avoiding heart disease.

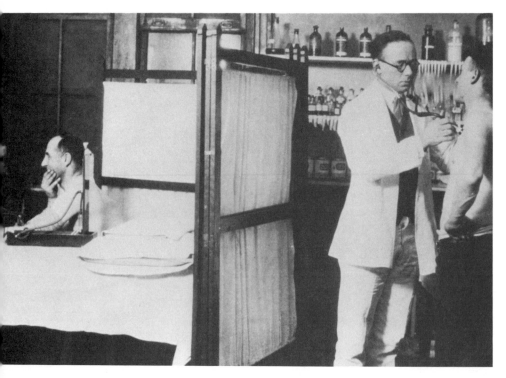

California at San Diego and other medical centers to test drugs that will prevent the brain damage that accompanies stroke and other head injuries. The drugs may not be able to restore a stroke survivor to his or her prestroke self but may improve such functional skills as walking and talking.

Improving blood circulation through the brain's blood vessels during stroke is essential to preventing extensive cell damage. An experimental drug, rt-PA, successfully used to open blocked blood vessels in heart attack patients, is now being tested in stroke patients.

New understanding of how brain cells behave during stroke has led to another treatment strategy. As brain cells die during stroke or injury, they release chemicals to neighboring cells that eventually cause the adjacent cells to die as well. Drugs under development include those that prevent dying cells from releasing this chemical message and those that prevent neighboring cells from receiving, amplifying, or retransmitting the chemical signal.

Boosting Natural Substances

Enzymes are proteins found in the human body, catalysts that make specific chemical reactions happen. The future may see large-scale production of these substances by transplanting their genetic instructions into living cells in the laboratory. Tissue plasminogen activator (TPA) and streptokinase are enzymes successfully being used to dissolve clots in blood vessels. In the June 1989 issue of *Nature*, Dr. Joseph Sambrook and his team at Texas Southwestern Medical Center reported successful adaptation of the TPA molecule so that it worked more effectively in the body.

Being able to produce human enzymes in large quantities and customize them is a promising direction. The same is true of gamma globulin, another class of blood protein that acts as an antibody and fights infection along with the immune system. Experiments are now under way in which gamma globulin is being used to help fight Kawasaki disease.

Lasers and Ultrasound

A study performed by Dr. Karl R. Karsch and associates at the Eberhard-Karls-University in the Federal Republic of Germany reported success in using a laser angioplasty method to remove plaque in coronary arteries. Dr. Sanjeev Saksena and his team at the Newark Beth Israel Medical Center in New Jersey and the University of Medicine and Dentistry of New Jersey–New Jersey Medical School in Newark have successfully treated arrhythmia by using lasers to remove abnormal sections of cardiac tissue (reported in the December 1, 1989, issue of the *American Journal of Cardiology*). Lasers may also provide an alternative to bypass surgery as a way to improve blood circulation in the heart.

Ultrasound may be another way to remove hardened deposits on valves that contribute to stenosis. Dr. Walter J. Scott and associates at the University of Chicago Medical Center reported in the November 15, 1989, issue of the *American Journal of Cardiology* their success in using ultrasound to break up deposits on the aortic valve as an alternative to entirely replacing the valve.

Many cardiovascular diseases can be prevented. Learning about the body and adopting a healthy life-style, combined with new advances in medical science, can result in a longer and healthier life.

•   •   •   •

APPENDIX:
FOR MORE INFORMATION

The following is a list of organizations that can provide further information on issues related to stroke and heart disease.

HEART DISEASE

American Heart Association
7320 Greenville Avenue
Dallas, TX 75231
(214) 889-7575
(214) 373-6300

American College of Cardiology
9111 Old Georgetown Road
Bethesda, MD 20814
(301) 897-5400

Canadian Heart Foundation
160 George Street
Suite 200
Ottawa, Ontario K1N 9M2
Canada
(613) 237-4361

The Coronary Club, Inc.
Cleveland Clinic Educational
 Foundation

9500 Euclid Avenue
Cleveland, OH 44120
(216) 444-3690

Heart Disease Research Foundation
 (cardiology)
50 Court Street
Brooklyn, NY 11201
(718) 649-6210

Mended Hearts, Inc.
7320 Greenville Avenue
Dallas, TX 75231
(214) 706-1442

National Heart, Lung, and Blood
 Institute
National Institutes of Health
9000 Rockville Pike, Building 31,
 Room 4A21
Bethesda, MD 20892
(301) 496-4236

HYPERTENSION

International Stress and Tension
  Control Association
Institute of Stress Management
U.S. International University
10455 Pomerado Road
San Diego, CA 92131
(619) 693-4669

National Hypertension Association
324 East 30th Street
New York, NY 10016
(212) 889-3557

STROKE

Canadian Stroke Recovery
  Association
170 The Donway West
Suite 122
Don Mills, Ontario M3C 2G3
Canada
(416) 441-1421

Stroke Club International
805 12th Street
Galveston, TX 77550
(409) 762-1022

FURTHER READING

American Medical Association. *The American Medical Association Book of Heartcare*. New York: Random House, 1984.

Barnard, Christiaan, and Peter Evans. *Your Healthy Heart*. New York: McGraw-Hill, 1985.

Becker, Gail L. *Heart Smart: A Plan for Low-Cholesterol Living*. New York: Simon & Schuster, 1985.

Cohn, Keith, and Darby Duke. *Coming Back: A Guide to Recovering from Heart Attack*. New York: Addison-Wesley, 1987.

Cohn, Peter F., and Joan K. Cohn. *Heart Talk: Preventing and Coping with Silent and Painful Heart Disease*. New York: Harcourt Brace Jovanovich, 1987.

Davis, Goode P. *The Heart: The Living Pump*. Washington, DC: U.S. News Books, 1981.

Donahue, Peggy Jo. *How to Prevent a Stroke*. Emmaus, PA: Rodale Press, 1989.

Rees, Michael K. *The Complete Guide to Living with High Blood Pressure*. New York: Prentice-Hall, 1988.

Roth, Eli M., and Sandra Streicher. *Good Cholesterol, Bad Cholesterol*. Rocklin, CA: Prima Publishing & Communications, 1989.

Rothfeder, Jeffrey. *Heart Rhythms*. Boston: Little, Brown, 1989.

Schacht, Richard A. *Understanding High Blood Pressure and Its Treatment*. Lexington, KY: Ricca, 1987.

Warren, James V., and Genell J. Subak-Sharpe. *Managing Hypertension*. New York: Doubleday, 1986.

———. *Surviving Your Heart Attack*. New York: Doubleday, 1984.

Wolinsky, Harvey, and Gary Ferguson. *The Heart Attack Recovery Handbook*. New York: Warner Books, 1988.

GLOSSARY

angiography an X-ray visualization of blood vessels or the heart after the injection of dye by catheterization

aorta the largest artery in the body; carries blood from the heart to be distributed by branch arteries throughout the body

aortic valve a valve connecting the left ventricle to the aorta

artery any of the muscular- and elastic-walled vessels that carry blood away from the heart through the body

arteriole any of the small branches of arteries that extend in a network to surrounding tissue

atrioventricular node (AV node) a small mass of tissue located in the wall of the right atrium, adjacent to the septum; passes impulses received from the sinoatrial node to the bundle of His

atrium a chamber, or passage, located on both the right and left sides in the upper half of the heart; receives blood from veins and then forces it into the ventricles

auscultation the act of listening to sounds arising from within the body, especially from organs such as the heart and lungs, for the purpose of detecting abnormalities

blood pressure the force exerted by the blood against the walls of any vessel

bundle of His a small band of fibers in the heart; conducts the sinoatrial node's impulse from the AV node to the right and left ventricles, where the bundle of His is continuous with the Purkinje fibers

capillary a microscopic blood vessel that links arterioles and venules and forms networks where oxygen in the blood is exchanged for carbon dioxide in the tissues of the body

cardiac catheterization a technique used in diagnosis and treatment of heart disorders; involves the passage of a small plastic tube into the heart through a blood vessel

cardiovascular disease illness of the heart and blood vessels

diastole the dilation of the cavities of the heart during which they fill with blood

echocardiography a diagnostic procedure that measures and records cardiac structure and functioning by bouncing high-frequency sound waves against the heart

electrocardiograph (EKG) a device that measures and records the electrical variations occurring during the heartbeat

invasive devices or diagnostic techniques, such as cardiac catheterization and angiography, that involve entry into the living body by incision or insertion of an instrument

magnetic resonance imaging (MRI) a scanning technique in which a specific area of the body is put into a magnetic field and exposed to different levels of radio frequency so that variations in energy emitted from the body when the frequency is turned off create a three-dimensional image

mitral valve (bicuspid valve) a valve composed of two triangular flaps, or cusps, located between the left atrium and left ventricle

myocardium the middle and thickest of the three muscle layers that compose the heart wall

noninvasive devices or diagnostic techniques, such as auscultation, echocardiography, electrocardiography, and magnetic resonance imaging, that do not require entry by incision or insertion of an instrument into the living body

pericardium the double-layered sac enclosing the heart and the roots of the great blood vessels originating from the heart; comprises an inner serous layer, an outer fibrous layer, and the pericardial cavity

pulmonary artery the artery that carries oxygen-depleted blood from the right ventricle of the heart to the lungs

pulmonary circulation the passage of venous, or oxygen-depleted, blood through the right atrium, right ventricle, and pulmonary arteries to the lungs, where it is oxygenated, and its return via the pulmonary veins to the left atrium of the heart

pulmonary valve a valve that connects the right ventricle to the pulmonary artery

septum a dividing wall or membrane; the muscular wall between the left and right sides of the heart

sinoatrial node (SA node) also known as the pacemaker; a small mass of tissue, located within the musculature of the right atrium, that initiates the pulses stimulating the heart

sphygmomanometer an instrument consisting of a gauge, cuff, and pump, used to measure blood pressure

stroke a decrease in or loss of consciousness sometimes followed by paralysis, resulting from the failure of a blood vessel and the subsequent destruction of brain tissue

systemic circulation the passage of oxygenated blood from the left side of the heart to the tissues and organs throughout the body via systemic arteries and the capillaries

systole the normal, rhythmic contraction of the heart, by which blood is circulated through the body

tricuspid valve a valve composed of three triangular flaps, or cusps, located between the right atrium and the right ventricle of the heart

vein any of the thin-walled vessels that carry blood from the body back to the heart

ventricle a small cavity located on both the right and left sides in the lower half of the heart; receives blood from the atrium and then contracts when filled, forcing the blood into the arteries

venule any of the small veins connecting the capillaries to the larger systemic veins

INDEX

PICTURE CREDITS

Anne Galperin is a free-lance writer on health issues, computers, and other subjects. She is a graduate of Northwestern University. She has worked as an associate editor for Macmillan Publishing Company and as a writer and reporter for *Windy City Times*, the nation's second-largest gay/lesbian newspaper. She has also served an internship at Old Orchard Psychiatric Hospital in Skokie, Illinois, tutoring disadvantaged teenagers.

Dale C. Garell, M.D., is medical director of California Children Services, Department of Health Services, County of Los Angeles. He is also associate dean for curriculum at the University of Southern California School of Medicine and clinical professor in the Department of Pediatrics & Family Medicine at the University of Southern California School of Medicine. From 1963 to 1974, he was medical director of the Division of Adolescent Medicine at Children's Hospital in Los Angeles. Dr. Garell has served as president of the Society for Adolescent Medicine, chairman of the youth committee of the American Academy of Pediatrics, and as a forum member of the White House Conference on Children (1970) and White House Conference on Youth (1971). He has also been a member of the editorial board of the *American Journal of Diseases of Children*.

C. Everett Koop, M.D., Sc.D., is former Surgeon General, Deputy Assistant Secretary for Health, and Director of the Office of International Health of the U.S. Public Health Service. A pediatric surgeon with an international reputation, he was previously surgeon-in-chief of Children's Hospital of Philadelphia and professor of pediatric surgery and pediatrics at the University of Pennsylvania. Dr. Koop is the author of more than 175 articles and books on the practice of medicine. He has served as surgery editor of the *Journal of Clinical Pediatrics* and editor-in-chief of the *Journal of Pediatric Surgery*, Dr. Koop has received nine honorary degrees and numerous other awards, including the Denis Brown Gold Medal of the British Association of Paediatric Surgeons, the William E. Ladd Gold Medal of the American Academy of Pediatrics, and the Copernicus Medal of the Surgical Society of Poland. He is a Chevalier of the French Legion of Honor and a member of the Royal College of Surgeons, London.